Captain Stanland's Journey

The North Midland Territorials go to War

This book is dedicated to the memory of the Territorial soldiers from Lincolnshire, Leicestershire, Nottinghamshire, Derbyshire and Staffordshire who served on the Western Front in the First World War, particularly to Captain Meaburn Staniland and his brother Second Lieutenant Geoffrey Staniland of the 4th Lincolns

Captain Staniland's Journey

THE NORTH MIDLAND TERRITORIALS GO TO WAR

MARTIN MIDDLEBROOK

LEO COOPER

Other books by Martin Middlebrook

The First Day on the Somme
The Nuremberg Raid
Convoy
Battleship (*with Patrick Mahoney*)
The Kaiser's Battle
The Battle of Hamburg
The Peenemünde Raid
The Schweinfurt-Regensburg Mission
The Bomber Command War Diaries (*with the late Chris Everitt*)
Operation Corporate
(*in paperback as* Task Force *and* The Falklands War)
The Berlin Raids
The Fight for the 'Malvinas'
The Somme Battlefields (with Mary Middlebrook)
Arnhem 1944
Your Country Needs You

Local Books for the History of Boston Project

Boston at War
The Catholic Church in Boston

First published in Great Britain in 2003
LEO COOPER
an imprint of
Pen & Sword Books Ltd
47 Church Street
Barnsley
South Yorkshire
S70 2AS

ISBN 0 85052 996 4 paperback
ISBN 1-84415-048-8 hardback

A CIP catalogue record for this book is
available from the British Library

Printed and bound in England by
CPI UK

CONTENTS

MAPS

Maps by Roni from preliminary drawings by Martin Middlebrook
Under The Messines Ridge, April-June 1915
The Ypres Salient, July-September 1915
Captain Staniland's Journey
Under The Messines Ridge Tour
Salient Sector Tour

PHOTOGRAPHS AND CEMETERY PLANS

Acknowledgements are due as follows: The Ringrose Law Group, page 12; the late Robert Staniland, page 14; Taylor Library, pages 20, 51, 54, 62, 65, 74, 91, 107; Museum of Lincolnshire Life, pages 25, 29, 33, 44, 47, 72; Michael Vansuyt, pages 27, 31; *The Sherwood Foresters in the Great War, The Robin Hoods*, page 39; Ieper Archives, pages 43, 52; Imperial War Museum, pages 53, 56, 66, 67, 134; the IWM references are: E(AUS)21313, Q49382, Q51177, Q17849, Q100816; Poperinghe Archives, page 59; Rear Admiral Geoffrey Hall, page 81; *5th South Staffords History*, page 97; Commonwealth War Graves Commission, pages 121, 122, 126, 133-4: Tijl Capoen, page 131.
Nearly all other photographs were taken by Mary (mostly) and Martin Middlebrook.

INTRODUCTION

'Jane. Why is your house called LINDENHOEK?'

This story began with that simple, idle enquiry of mine when collecting my wife from a visit to her friend's home in Boston. 'Oh. That was where Tom's father met the body of Captain Staniland being brought back for burial.' 'Tom' was Tom Kent, Jane's late husband. Tom's father, it was explained, was William Kent who survived the war and returned to the family business of monumental masons located close to Boston Cemetery on Horncastle Road. When William Kent and his wife had a new house built next to the business premises in the late 1920s, Mr Kent decided to name it LINDENHOEK. The nameplate is now on another house in Boston in which his daughter-in-law, my wife's friend Jane, now lives.

I knew about Captain Meaburn Staniland, the commander of Boston's pre-war infantry Territorial company. He had taken the company to war in 1915 and was killed later in the year. I have seen his grave in Dranoutre, a village seven miles south-west of Ypres. William Kent was a lance corporal in the company; my uncle, my mother's eldest brother, was one of the company's sergeants. 'Lindenhoek', however, I did not recognize, despite having visited the Ypres area many times. I thought Lindenhoek might be the pre-war Belgian name for Sanctuary Wood close to where Captain Staniland was killed; modern maps show a farm named Lindenhof near the southern end of the wood. An enquiry to the helpful Ieper Tourist Office brought a correction. Lindenhoek was, and still is, a small place more than nine miles away by road from Sanctuary Wood. It is just east of Mont Kemmel and just south of Kemmel village. 'Linden' – 'lime tree' – is an easy translation; 'hoek', according to the Tourist Office, means "corner" in Flemish – a small area, a hamlet, mostly located at crossroads'. There are many place names in Flanders ending in 'hoek'.

Dranoutre, where Captain Staniland is buried, is a mile and a half further on from Lindenhoek. Why had his body been brought so far from where he died? Why had Lance Corporal Kent gone to Lindenhoek to meet the body? Why had that meeting made such a deep impression on him that he later named his new house after that little 'corner' of Belgium?

Finding the answers to those questions led me to research of a most interesting nature. Initially, it was just a personal project, but it developed in ever increasing circles until I found that what I was really studying was the experiences of a whole Territorial division in its first year of the war – six months of preparation in England, six months at the front in Belgium. Those six months in Belgium – April to September 1915 – would split neatly into two halves on different sectors. They would also encompass exactly the

7

front line service of my uncle. Pen and Sword Books thought that the subject could be turned into a book. It will not be a work of sweeping military history or a description of a great battle; I retired from such writing ten years ago. Critics may call it a hybrid book and they will be partially correct. It is part family history, part local history, particularly for Boston and Lincolnshire, but also in lesser degree for the counties of Leicestershire, Nottinghamshire, Derbyshire and Staffordshire which sent their Territorials off to fight with the Lincolns in 1914. It is also a modest contribution to military history. Not many books describe in detail a prolonged period of the simple trench-holding duty that occupied the majority of the time for soldiers on the Western Front in the First World. This is told here mainly through the experiences of one battalion – the 4th Lincolns – but these were typical of the introduction to war of all of the North Midland battalions. Finally, there are descriptions of cemeteries in areas not on the popular battlefield touring routes which may interest enthusiasts of that activity.

I am pleased to have been able to study part of that year of 1915. It was not a popular one in which to die. To have a relative killed at Mons, Le Cateau or on the Marne or Aisne in 1914 has rarity value. The Somme and Passchendaele in 1916 and 1917 are the celebrity battles. The last year, 1918, with its massive offensives and sweeping advances of both sides, was the year of the conscript and of confusion. A grandfather killed at Neuve-Chapelle, Festubert or Loos in 1915 may arouse a flicker of interest, but to die at Peckham Corner or Armagh Wood in that year does not attract much attention. However that man is just as dead and the manner of his passing is just as worthy of remembrance.

That is one purpose of my telling the story of Lance Corporal Kent and Captain Staniland.

PART ONE

August 1914 to February 1915

The Territorials

The Territorial Force (later the Territorial Army) was only six years old when war broke out in August 1914. The Haldane Reforms of the Army in 1908 had brought the long established 'Volunteers' more closely into the county regiment system and given them a new name. But the role for these part-time soldiers remained the same; if the Regulars had to go overseas in time of war, the Territorial Force was to be deployed on Home Defence.

Lincolnshire had possessed two Volunteer battalions. The 2nd Volunteers, covering the southern part of this large county, became the 4th Battalion of the Lincolnshire Regiment – the 4th Lincolns for short. The battalion was part of a fully Territorial division organized entirely on Regular Army lines. The 4th Lincolns formed a brigade with the 5th Lincolns, from the north of the county, and the 4th and 5th Leicesters. A second brigade was formed from two battalions each from Nottinghamshire and Derbyshire which had a combined county regiment known as the Sherwood Foresters. The third brigade was made up of two battalions each of the South and the North Staffordshires. The division's artillery, engineer and other support units were also provided by Territorials from throughout the region. The whole formed the North Midland Division, one of fourteen such Territorial infantry divisions created by Haldane in 1908.

One aspect of the Haldane Reforms had not been implemented in the Territorials. While the old eight company organization of Regular battalions had been changed to one of four larger companies in 1908, the Territorials still retained their eight companies. The 4th Lincolns' companies were based as follows:

'A' Company	Lincoln
'B' Company	Grantham
'C' Company	Boston
'D' Company	Stamford
'E' Company	Lincoln
'F' Company	Spalding
'G' Company	Horncastle
'H' Company	Lincoln.

The Battalion Commander was Lieutenant Colonel John Jessop, a doctor

The North Midland Division, Territorial Force

LINCOLNS AND LEICESTERS BRIGADE

4th Battalion Lincolnshire Regiment | 5th Battalion Lincolnshire Regiment | 4th Battalion Leicestershire Regiment | 5th Battalion Leicestershire Regime...

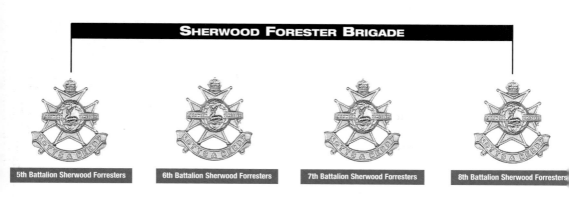

SHERWOOD FORESTER BRIGADE

5th Battalion Sherwood Forresters | 6th Battalion Sherwood Forresters | 7th Battalion Sherwood Forresters | 8th Battalion Sherwood Forresters

STAFFORDSHIRE BRIGADE

5th Battalion South Staffordshires | 6th Battalion South Staffordshires | 5th Battalion North Staffordshires | 6th Battalion North Staffordshires

in general practice in Horncastle but whose home was in Woodhall Spa. The only Regulars were a full-time adjutant at Battalion Headquarters at Lincoln and a sergeant instructor, usually a long service man, at each of the drill halls. All other personnel were the part-time volunteers who signed on for four years and had to attend an annual training camp each summer and evening and weekend 'drills'. Otherwise, they lived normal civilian lives. Each man joined as a private but could re-engage for further terms of service and, as the example of Lieutenant Colonel Jessop had shown, could be promoted and rise right up to that rank.

Territorial soldiering was not a popular occupation in most parts of the country. The Territorial Force nationally was one-third below establishment in August 1914, however, the Boston Company was almost at full strength providing an outlet for young men's energy, enthusiasm and initiative, and for the widespread patriotism of the period. A fine new drill hall in Main Ridge had been built and formally opened in 1913, with the long speeches by notables common to such occasions. The chairman of proceedings was Lord Kesteven and Major-General Bethune, Director General of the Territorial Force, performed the actual opening ceremony. The building had cost £1,800 to construct and boasted a large drill area, the orderly officers' room, a sergeants' room and a thirty yards long miniature rifle range.

BOSTON'S NEW TERRITORIAL DRILL-HALL.

County Association's Building in Mainridge Opened by General Bethune.

IMPOSING MILITARY PARADE: COLOURS AND SILVER KEY, AND MANY VISITING OFFICERS.

Lord Kesteven Presides, and Speaks at Dinner and Smoking Concert.

THE NEW DRILL HALL.

The standard of musketry was high and competition was keen. There was a proper outdoor rifle range in the countryside at the side of the River Witham (the site of it is now beneath the municipal refuse disposal site.)

I must declare a personal interest both in the opening of the drill hall and in the rifle shooting. The newspaper report of the opening (*Lincolnshire Standard*, 3 October 1913) shows that Sergeant Instructor Stephens and my uncle, Sergeant Crick, were responsible for preparing the decorations, and prominent in the printed list of guests were my grandmother and two aunts. My mother, aged only nine, was apparently deemed too young to be invited.

As for rifle shooting, I possess a silver cup presented by 'The Officers of the Company' in 1907 to Private A. Crick for winning that year's company shooting competition and an exhibit in the Royal Lincolnshire Regiment

Meaburn Staniland, prominent citizen, solicitor and Town Clerk of Boston.

section of the Museum of Lincolnshire Life is a rifle described as a 'Lee-Enfield .303 Sniper Target Rifle'. A small brass plate on the butt is inscribed: 'Presented by the London Small Arms Co. Ltd. Won by Sergeant A. Crick, 4th Lincolnshire'. The records of the National Rifle Association at Bisley show that he came first in a competition for Territorial soldiers 'Associated with the Second Stage of the "Queen Mary's" Prize Competition' fired over distances of 500 to 100 yards using fifty shots. The entrance fee was five shillings; my uncle won the first of four prize rifles and the top money prize of £5. Two other Lincolnshire Territorials appear in the list of prize winners – Lance Sergeant H. Gibbons and Lance Corporal J. A. Clarke, both of the 5th Battalion from the north of the county, appearing at Numbers 27 and 30 in the list and winning £1 each. Both men appear to have survived the coming war.

The Boston Territorials may have been close to full strength on the outbreak of war but it was out of balance in its ranks. It contained more than twenty NCOs, about a hundred privates, but only three officers. Captain Meaburn Staniland was the company commander but there were only two subalterns – Second Lieutenants Harold Marris and Edward (Ted) Beaulah, the one a solicitor, the other a young medical student. There was another Boston officer, Major Oliver Cooper, a corn merchant, but he was too senior to command a company and was one of two majors on the staff of Lieutenant Colonel Jessop.

Much attention should be focussed on Captain Staniland; he will be the central character of this story. Meaburn Staniland was a member of an influential and wealthy family in Boston. The wealth had come into the family from the marriage of a lady to a Staniland of an earlier generation. She was from a rich coal mine-owning family in Yorkshire. That lady also introduced 'Meaburn' – pronounced 'Mayburn' – into the family. The name was used frequently as a Christian name for boys through several generations. The present Meaburn's grandfather – another Meaburn – had been one of Boston's two MPs in the 1860s. The MP's son, Lieutenant Colonel Robert Staniland, had been the commander of the 2nd Volunteer Battalion and was now head of one of the town's leading law practices. He had once been town clerk, a much sought after part-time appointment. He was also Chairman of the Boston School Board and it had named a new primary school after him. The Staniland family was certainly influential as even a century later, long after the last of the family had left the town, it is still remembered by a Staniland School and a Staniland Road.

The Territorial officer, Meaburn Staniland, Robert's son, had a brother and three sisters, had attended Rugby School, was also a solicitor and was now, at thirty-four years old, the youngest town clerk in England. He was happily married – a bishop had officiated at the wedding – and had four small sons, two of them twins. The youngest son – yet another Meaburn – was only six weeks old on the outbreak of war. The family lived in an elegant residence – Wyberton House – in the village of the same name just outside Boston. Captain Staniland's part-time military service went back a long way. As a private in the Volunteers he had been one of eight Boston men chosen to go to South Africa to reinforce the 2nd Lincolns in the Boer War. They were known in the town as 'The Gallant Eight'; Oliver Cooper had been another of the 'Eight'. One man had died of enteric fever but the others returned safely, all to be granted the Freedom of the Borough. Private Staniland, as he was then, had been commended for bravery for helping to save the horses of the Scots Greys under fire in the engagement at Nitral's Nek. He was then rapidly promoted, became a qualified musketry instructor, and was commissioned in 1902.

It would be hard to find a more celebrated or influential citizen in his home town than Captain Meaburn Staniland in that month of August 1914. A man in his prime, at the peak of personal, professional and public life, and commanding a company of what some would say were the best and most patriotic of the town's young men ready for wartime duty.

The Outbreak of War

Rumblings of war in early August 1914 caught the Boston Territorials at their annual camp, held that year at Bridlington. An early return on 3 August – Bank Holiday Monday – brought the companies of the battalion back to their home town drill halls to await events. War was declared next

Captain Staniland, Territorial Company Commander.

day and the part-time soldiers immediately became full-time ones. The companies of the 4th Lincolns marched off to reform the battalion at Lincoln and eventually the whole of the North Midland Division assembled in and around Luton.

Major changes were taking place that would transform the future of the Territorials. Lord Kitchener, the new Secretary of State for War, anticipated a long conflict, contrary to the popular view of 'all over by Christmas', and was granted powers by Parliament to create what was a huge Army by British standards for service in the war being waged by the all-conscript armies on the Continent. He would raise a completely new force of no less than thirty new infantry divisions, but this 'New Army' would be formed within the Regular Army system and its oft-told story does not concern this narrative. But Kitchener also wanted a substantial further contribution from the Territorial Force. He appealed to its men to volunteer for overseas service and he also ordered the raising of a duplicate 'Second Line' of fourteen more Territorial divisions.

These were decisions of an amazing nature for the Territorial soldiers. In the last war, just eight volunteers from Boston had been allowed to go to South Africa. Now every man at Luton had to decide whether to offer his services for overseas duty. It was not clear whether that service would be for garrison duty abroad to replace the Regulars being brought back to England, or to one of the fighting fronts. The Western Front, where the British Expeditionary Force was fighting hard at Mons, the Retreat, the Marne and Ypres, seemed the likely destination.

The decisions were soon made. A total of 116 Boston Company men of all ranks, including the three officers, volunteered. It is not known how many men declined for various personal or family reasons; the national average was about 10 per cent. The Boston Artillery Battery produced even more men for overseas service, 144 men including five officers, and the small Yeomanry Troop a further ten men. Group photographs of the willing men were taken and the Boston Guardian produced a commemorative poster of the three proud groups.

The men who did not volunteer returned to their home towns, not to be released but to help train Kitchener's Second Line Territorial units for which a steady flow of new men was coming forward to enlist at the drill halls. Under new terms of service, these new men were all obliged to serve overseas if required, but the pre-war men who had returned from Luton were still deemed to be 'Home Service' men and they could remain so throughout the war, even in the later years of conscription, a concession that would sometimes cause bitterness among the families of pre-war Territorials who lost their lives on foreign service.

The creation of the Second Line meant that the 4th Lincolns at Luton now became the 'First 4th Lincolns' and the new battalion at home was the 'Second 4th'; these would be abbreviated to 1/4th and 2/4th. Every unit in the North Midland Division was affected in this way. It became officially the 1st North Midland Division, with a completely new Second Line division forming back in the North Midland counties.

Preparing for Action

The War Office was in a state of turmoil in those first months of the war, supporting the efforts of the British Expeditionary Force now fighting desperately on the Western Front at the same time as it was creating Kitchener's new divisions at home. The first of the New Army divisions would not be ready for active service until well into 1915, but there were fourteen Territorial divisions, already formed and equipped, with their men reasonably well trained and eager to overseas. The War Office dealt with the Territorials in three different ways. Six divisions were forced to give up the best of their battalions, which were sent out immediately to reinforce the hard-pressed BEF at Ypres; these divisions would not be available for overseas duty as complete divisions for a considerable time. Three divisions were chosen for immediate dispatch to overseas garrison duty to replace the

Boston Territorials for Foreign Service.

"C" COMPANY, 4th BATTALION, LINCOLNSHIRE REGIMENT.

Photo by]

[W. H. Cox, 2, Wellingtch-street, Luton.

Row 1 [from left to right].—Ptes. Johnson, Allm, P. W. Day, E. Bridgeman, R. Wright, Watson, Clark, and Pinner, Lance-Corpl. Bishop, Lance-Corpl. Smith, Pte. Carter, Pte. G. W. Holmes, Lance-Corpl. H. Clark, Ptes. R. Meeds, W. Wamlawell, W. West, H. Brind, Hunt, and Lance-Corpl. Bannister.

Row 2.—Ptes. G. W. Clarke, Hayward, Woodham, Lee, Caburn, Crawford, Dixon, Davies, F. Day, Robinson, Wilson, J. Foster, Chester, and H. Darby.

Row 3.—Pte. J. R. Parker, Pte. G. Barsby, Lance-Corpl. Allison, Pte. Goodacre, Pte. Coe, Pte. F. Lilley, Lance-Corpl. Greswell, Lance-Corpl. Cannon, Ptes. Dallywater, Ormesby, Whelbourn, W. Parvin, H. Leafe, and F. Brook.

Row 4.—Ptes. H. Hall, Mason, J. Sharpe, J. Gorner, H. Barsby, W. E. Sharpe, G. Marris, Elston, Lance-Corpl. Wilkes, Ptes. Johnson, Barber, G. Bear, Houghton, Haw, Bannister, Donnington, Rogers, S. Thompson, J. Pocklington, and Chamberlain.

Row 5.—Ptes. Short, W. Horry, Chier G. Holland, Seargall, Maddison, Maltby, Given, Kent, Baker, Lance-Corpl. Rasen, Pte. G. Martin, Lance-Corpl. Wakefield, Pte. C. J. Mawson, Ptes. Airey, Naylor, G. Botterill, and Chamberlain.

Row 6.—Pte. Cousens, Corpl. Barchmall, Lance-Corpl. F. Waite, Sergt. A. Crick, Lance-Sergt. Bailey, Sergt. R. Parker, Colr.-Sergt. G. Stephens, Second Lieut. E. A. Beajah, Capt. M. Staniland (commanding "C" Company), Major O. Cooper, Second Lieut. H. C. Marris, Colr.-Sergt. A. Paul, Sergt. Johnson, Sergt. Sawyer, Corpl. Holmes, Corpl. Hand, Lance-Corpl. Wilcox, Pte. Christy, Pte. J. Parker.

Row 7.—Ptes. S. Whelbourn, J. S. Perkins, Teegus, Corpl. Tomlinson, Ptes. Overton, Forman, Ulyatt, Mitcham, J. West, H. Grocock, H. Reynolds, East, Wortley, and Plumridge.

Regulars being brought home to form new active service divisions. The remaining five Territorial divisions remained intact at home, continuing their training and awaiting further orders.

At the end of October 1914 the 1st North Midland Division was warned for overseas service, though the destination was not stated, and the men were sent home on embarkation leave. However the order was cancelled. It can be seen now that the destination would probably have been garrison duty in India, but another division was obviously chosen instead. There followed a move, but only a short one, the 1/4th Lincolns to Bishop's Stortford in Essex, the 1/5th Lincolns to nearby Stansted. Christmas passed with no further orders.

Some reorganization took place. In January an order came that Territorial battalions were finally to abandon their eight company organization and comply with the Regulars' four company system. In the 1/4th Lincolns, the Lincoln itself, Boston, Grantham and Stamford were selected as the strongest companies to which men from the disbanded companies would be attached. The old Boston Company became 'A' Company, taking in most of the old Spalding Company and possibly some from the small Horncastle Company, which was completely dispersed. This, following on from the departure of the Home Service men the previous autumn, represented steps in a steady process of the loss of the pre-war character, not only of the Lincolns but also of every Territorial battalion. Letters home and reports in local papers would continue to refer to the 'Boston Company' or the 'Spalding Company' for some time, even though they no longer existed, but Boston was fortunate in that its men all continued to serve in the same company, with Captain Staniland remaining in command. The new double-strength company still remained as a captain's command, unlike the Second World War when infantry companies were commanded by a major. One grumble at the locations where the battalions were continuing their training was that the old company form of drill was replaced by a new platoon drill.

The delay in proceeding to a new duty provided the opportunity for some changes in personnel. To replace the departed Home Service men and bring the company up to full strength, some of the wartime volunteers arrived from the Second Line at Boston. There was no shortage of such men. At a time when volunteers in the industrial areas were rushing to form the Pals battalions of the New Army, the response in the rural counties was more evenly balanced. Statistics available for recruitment up to the end of November 1914 show that, in the North Midland counties, 42 per cent of wartime volunteers in Leicestershire and 39 per cent in Lincolnshire joined the Territorials; these were among the highest proportions in Britain. By contrast, the Nottinghamshire and Derbyshire rate was 28 per cent and that of Staffordshire 25 per cent.*

---

* The statistics are from *Britons, To Arms!, The Story of the British Volunteer Soldier*, by Glenn A. Steppler, Alan Sutton Publishing, 1992.

Pre-war Boston NCOs. In the front row, Sergeant Sawyer on the left survived the war; Colour Sergeants Stephens and Paul volunteered for overseas service but were deemed too old and had to stay behind to train recruits. In the back row, Corporal Burchnall and Sergeants Crick, Parker and Bailey were all killed at the Front in 1915.

There were promotions for some of the pre-war men. Colour-Sergeant George Stephens, earlier the Company Instructor Sergeant, was promoted to Company Sergeant Major and was willing to go overseas despite his advanced age, but orders came that he was to return to Boston and help train new recruits. He would be a captain within a year and eventually a major! The depot at Lincoln provided a replacement; he was Company Sergeant Major Peasgood, probably a senior Regular sergeant promoted to look after these Territorials.

The Boston Company had been short of officers. Second Lieutenant Harold Marris was promoted to full lieutenant, probably becoming the company's Second in Command. He was married in January to the daughter of the vicar of Leverton, the wedding 'attended by Lieutenant Colonel Jessop and the officers of the 4th Batt Lincs Regt' according to the *Lincolnshire Standard*. Four new second lieutenants were created. The first was Captain Staniland's brother, Geoffrey. He had earlier been a Volunteer but not a Territorial. He had applied for a commission in the Lincolns on the outbreak of war, hoping to join his brother. He was accepted, but a clerk in the War Office made a mistake and commissioned him in the 4th Londons, not Lincolns. The error was soon corrected. Two privates who had only joined the Boston Company on the outbreak of war were also commissioned; they were Geoffrey Marris, brother of Lieutenant Harold Marris, and Alexander Crawford. Finally, Basil Wood who had joined the Territorials in Boston on the outbreak of war and been commissioned into the 2/4th Lincolns, was transferred to the 1/4th. The four new officers had one thing in common – the law. Geoffrey Staniland and Alexander Crawford were both qualified solicitors and Basil Wood was articled to a Boston legal firm. Geoffrey Marris was a farmer but was the brother of a solicitor. It would be reasonable to assume that, with six of the seven officers in what was still basically the Boston Company associated with the town's legal profession, some favouritism was taking place and this may have been so. None of the more experienced sergeants from the commercial class was promoted in this way. However it should be pointed out that all of the new officers had probably attended public schools where there were Officer Training Corps specifically set up under the 1908 Haldane Reforms to train young men as potential junior officers. Second Lieutenant Crawford did not remain long with the Boston Company, transferring to the 14th Sherwood Foresters and then to the 17th West Yorks – the 2nd Leeds Pals – with whom, as a captain, he was killed at Laventie. He is buried in St Vaast Post Cemetery, Plot 3, Row F. The other officers all went abroad with the 1/4th Lincolns.

The time for the next move was nigh. The King inspected the whole division on 25 February 1915. Captain Staniland's company stood at full strength with about 170 officers and men, of whom about 120 were from Boston. Orders for embarkation came a few days later. Once more the men went home to say their farewells. This time there was no cancellation. The division had been chosen as the first complete Territorial division to proceed to a fighting front – the Western Front. It was still designated officially as the 1st North Midland Division and its brigades as the Staffordshire, Lincolnshire-Leicestershire and Sherwood Forester Brigades. Kitchener was giving priority in bestowing official division numbering to his thirty New Army divisions and, although the North Midland Division was off to war before any of the New Army divisions, the War Office had not yet got round to numbering the Territorial divisions and brigades.

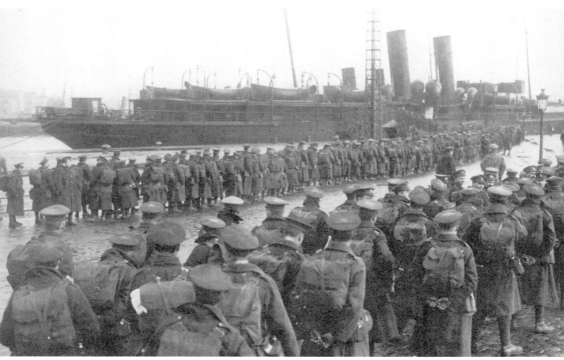

Troops waiting to board a cross-channel ferry for Le Havre.

Territorials in a quiet part of the line.

PART TWO

On Active Service

The North Midland Division landed at Le Havre in the last days of February 1915. The 1/4th Lincolns moved by train to the Cassel area in wintry weather; one of their horses died on the rail journey. They were fortunate in arriving when no major battles were taking place, so they were not rushed into action, and went into billets for nearly a week. General Horace Smith-Dorrien, the hero of Mons and the Retreat, inspected them. As a special role was being considered for it, the division did not proceed immediately to the front. The Battle of Neuve-Chapelle was being planned and the whole of the North Midland Division moved south, standing by to be a force of pursuit if the German line at Neuve-Chapelle should be captured. This was a naïve High Command theory; that fresh troops untainted by the staleness of static trench warfare were best suited for this role. But there was no breakthrough at Neuve-Chapelle and the division was not required there. It was a fortunate escape. When the same idea was used at the Battle of Loos in September, a similar role was allocated to two recently arrived New Army divisions. The result was a disaster.

The North Midland Division moved back north and was allowed a gentler introduction to the front line. Platoons were attached to battalions of the 4th Division on the quiet sector between Ploegsteert and Armentières, astride the frontier between Belgium and France. The 1/4th Lincolns were billeted in Ploegsteert – 'Plugstreet' to the soldiers – and received their trench instruction from the 1st Somerset Light Infantry and the London Rifle Brigade, the latter battalion being Territorials who had been rushed out to support the BEF the previous autumn and who were now considered veterans. The 1/4th Lincolns suffered their first casualties, just two men wounded. Others were not so fortunate. The 1/5th Leicesters suffered the first fatal battle casualty in the division when Lieutenant George Aked was hit in the head by a stray bullet while with the 2nd Essex on 5 March, his first day in the trenches, and died. The following day the Sherwood Foresters suffered their first death when Corporal C W T Sheppard of the 1/7th Battalion – the Nottingham City Battalion known as 'The Robin Hoods' – was accidentally shot by an NCO of the instructing battalion, the 1st Hampshires. The first Lincolnshire death did not occur until 29 March, when Corporal Harry Clarke of the 1/5th Lincolns, from Louth, was killed by enemy fire while attached to the 2nd East Lancashires in Ploegsteert

Wood. Lieutenant Aked is buried in Calvaire (Essex) Military Cemetery, Plot 1, Row H; Corporals Sheppard and Clarke are both buried in Lancashire Cottage Cemetery, Plot 1, Row F.

The North Midland Division moved a short distance north and took over its own sector early in April. I relieved the British 28th Division, comprised of Regular battalions brought back from overseas stations and which, having spent a few quiet weeks here, was now off to the more active Ypres Salient. The North Midland sector was a stretch about two and a half miles long directly facing the Messines Ridge. British troops had fought hard to retain the high ground of the ridge the previous autumn, but French troops had then taken over and been forced off it during the winter. Now the British were back, having to hold the makeshift line made by the French at the foot of the ridge. The Germans were above them with the advantage of good observation, not only of the trenches, but also of much of the ground in the British rear. It would not be an easy sector for the incoming troops to hold. There were no reserve units behind the North Midland Division and only a makeshift front line was stopping the Germans breaking through and outflanking Ypres from the south or, indeed, pushing straight on towards the Channel ports. A common saying in 1915 was that the Germans held their trenches with machine-gunners and the French with artillery protection. But the British had few machine-guns and early 1915 was the

German view southeastwards from their line at Spanbroekmolen on the Messines Ridge. The British front line, held first by the Sherwood Foresters then by the Lincolns-Leicesters, was less than 100 yards away, this side of the cows in the photograph. Many of the farms in the middle distance were North Midland reserve positions. The clearly visible villages of Wulverghem (one and a quarter miles away) and Neuve Eglise (two and a half miles) were in the Staffords' sector.

The dominating German position on the ridge as seen from the Staffords' front line near Messines village. The German front line was approximately where the cows are. The New Zealand Memorial on the left and the Irish Tower on the right commemorate the successful British advance two years later.

height of the great British shell-shortage crisis. Because of these factors, the saying went on, 'the British hold their trenches with men'. That flimsy line under the Messines Ridge had to be fully manned at all times. It was the first time a complete Territorial division had held a front-line sector and events would be watched by the High Command with much interest. Three other Territorial divisions went into trenches at about the same time: the London, South Midland and West Riding divisions took over similarly quiet sectors further south, in France. The next division to deploy was not so fortunate. The Northumbrian Division arrived just as the Germans launched the first gas attack north of Ypres and the Northumbrian battalions were thrown piecemeal into the desperate defence there. They suffered severe casualties and lost a high proportion of their pre-war Territorials in their first few days of action.

The North Midland Division was fortunate – no earlier loss of its individual units, no immediate pitched battle, just that gradual introduction of the whole pre-war division to the line. Its duty would be to man the front on a permanent basis, but there was much hard manual work also to be done. The front line was in soggy ground into which it was not possible to dig deep trenches and the 'trenches' were mainly sandbagged breastworks which the French had left in poor condition. The front line was not even continuous in many places, merely intermittent stretches of those breastworks furthermore, there were no support lines and no communication trenches. To remedy these deficiencies would be the main task of the North Midland men in the coming weeks; there would be more navvying than fighting. Each brigade was allocated a third of the divisional front, the Sherwood Foresters the north, the Lincolns and Leicesters the centre, the Staffordshires the south. Billeting villages about four miles in the rear, hidden from German observation, would be homes for battalions when not taking turns in the line. The routes between these villages and the front would become very familiar to the soldiers who would have to tramp them innumerable times. They will also be important to our story.

The sector may have had its disadvantages but it could have been far worse. Much of the BEF further south found itself in ugly coalmining areas of Northern France. This sector was in the most pleasant of gentle, Belgian countryside, and summer was coming.

The North Midland Territorials came to this duty with great enthusiasm. They had a strong bond of comradeship and high morale, were well trained in the skills in their pre-war training manuals – musketry, the company in attack and defence, construction of field fortifications – but they were really naïve novices in the different skills required for routine trench holding in this unexpected static warfare where their professional enemy were hardly ever seen. The result would sometimes be a careless disregard for danger, two extreme examples of this would be seen in coming months. There was also an unreadiness to embrace the strict disciplines of trench hygiene and this would produce a steady flow of casualties through sickness. The inability of some of the older, long service Volunteers and Territorials to stand the strain of prolonged duty in the trenches would be the cause of further loss. It would be the younger, tougher, more adaptable men who would emerge to lead the battalions in the subsequent periods of service.

Holding the Line

The North Midland Division would spend three months on this first trench sector. The infantry battalions would become familiar with every yard of trench, every lane, every track, every tumbled building in their brigade area. There were always the Germans in their trenches only fifty to a hundred yards ahead on the higher ground, held, it was thought, by Bavarian troops. There were a few farms – roofless close to the line, but mostly intact, if a little battered, in the immediate rear. Earlier British units

Officers, mainly 1/4th Lincolns, in the trenches in May 1915. Left is an RE officer, possibly Lieutenant Gosling killed in the E1 Left mine action later in May. Bottom is probably Lieuteant C. Ellwood, killed 2 June. The officer at top cannot be firmly identified. Centre are Majors Barrell and Cooper, both of whom later commanded the battalion. Right is young Second Lieutenant Newton who survived to reach the rank of lieutenant colonel. Note the mass of sandbags in the breastworks, a feature of the trenches in this area.

had christened most of the farms with English names that became official and would appear permanently on Army maps. Places such as Pond Farm, Frenchman's Farm and Packhorse Farm were all in the Lincolns' and Leicesters' brigade area. There were no villages near the front line. The nearest community was the hamlet of Lindenhoek, with no more than six or eight houses, some of them 'cabarets'- small cafés. Lindenhoek was a mile and a half behind the trenches. To the north, just inside the Sherwood

Foresters' sector, was the large village of Kemmel with the towering hill of the same name just behind it. All these places were under German observation.

Tours of duty in the trenches were normally of four days and nights duration. The division decided upon a 'pairing' system whereby a brigade allocated half of its frontage to two battalions which then took turn and turn about to hold the front line. The 1/4th Lincolns were paired with the 1/5th Leicesters and were allocated the left half of their brigade's frontage. The 1/5th Leicesters were a battalion of similar nature to the 1/4th Lincolns; they came from the country areas of their county with their pre-war Battalion HQ at Loughborough. The men from South Lincolnshire would share many a moment with the men from the towns and villages of Leicestershire in the coming months. The North Lincolnshire men, the 1/5th Battalion, were paired with the 1/4th Leicesters who came from the city of Leicester and its immediate surroundings. In theory, the battalions changed places in the darkness every four nights and so had equal periods of trench duty and rest at their billets in the rear. But, as a battalion could not leave the front line until properly relieved, a proportion of its time 'out of the line' was spent on the wearying four-mile approach and withdrawal marches along lanes, tracks or later, when they had been dug or constructed, long communication trenches – all with the heavy packs and rifles that were the infantryman's constant burden.

The front-line sector allocated to the brigade was almost directly opposite the furthermost point of the German-held salient on the Messines Ridge. The 1/4th Lincolns and 1/5th Leicesters spent their first trench tours just south of the apex of the salient, opposite a place where the German trenches ran through a peacetime crossroads called Kruisstraathoek. The 1/5th Leicesters took first turn here and were relieved by the 1/4th Lincolns on the night of 9 April. The Leicesters suffered their first two fatal casualties on that tour – Privates John Goode from Hinckley and William Harmer from Market Harborough. The Lincolns would suffer more heavily on their first tour but their casualties will be described later. Two companies occupied the front line, the mostly Boston 'A' Company having the doubtful honour of being one of these on that first tour. In the absence of a support line, the other two companies occupied three farms behind the line as reserve positions: Cooker's Farm, Pond Farm and Packhorse Farm. Battalion HQ and the Regimental Aid Post were at a further farm – Frenchman's Farm. The Lincolns and Leicesters shared four consecutive trench tours here.

On the night of 10 May there was then a leftward readjustment of frontages when the 1/4th Lincolns took over trenches from the 1/5th Sherwood Foresters. The Lincolns and Leicesters then held trenches slightly north of the easternmost point of the ridge for three trench tours each. Here, just behind the German line, were the ruins of a windmill called Spanbroekmolen and of another small cabaret café. 'Spanbroek' was an old Flemish dialect word that described a pair of French pantaloon trousers; 'molen' is a mill. A little to the north, and still on that same battalion frontage, the German line ran through a road junction which some London soldiers had earlier christened Peckham Corner. The German soldiers in the trenches between Spanbroekmolen and Peckham Corner were actually the most westerly members of their army in the entire stretch of front from well north of Ypres down to Armentières just over the French border to the south. Finally, on 2 June, the 1/5th Leicesters took over trenches from the Sherwood Foresters on the left again, with the Leicesters and Lincolns doing two tours each in a confused group of trenches opposite the German line between Peckham Corner and a small wood named, not surprisingly, Petit Bois. These northward adjustments of the allocated sectors were probably intended to thicken up the defence of the North Midland Division's left flank, the one closest to Ypres and thus more vulnerable to a German flanking attack on that vital place.

The pre-war mill on the Spanbroek spur of the Messines Ridge.

In total, the 1/4th Lincolns and 1/5th Leicesters each served nine trench tours in this general area between 5 April and 21 June, each battalion spending forty days and nights under the danger of enemy fire before the whole division was moved to a completely new sector. And all the time the other battalions in the brigade, the 1/5th Lincolns and 1/4th Leicesters, kept their watch, manning the trenches alongside on the right. The pairing of battalions in the other brigades were as follows: the 1/5th and 1/7th Sherwood Foresters – recruited in Derby City and Nottingham City respectively; 1/6th and 1/8th Sherwood Foresters – from the Derbyshire and Nottinghamshire towns; 1/5th and 1/6th South Staffords – from the Walsall and Wolverhampton areas; 1/5th and 1/6th North Staffords – from Stoke-on-Trent and the other Pottery towns and from Burton-on-Trent.

Those nine trench tours for each battalion were interspersed with an equal number of so-called rest periods at places about four miles behind the lines which were concealed from German observation by folds in the ground or by woods. In theory, those places were still within the range of German shells, but the Germans seem to have had few long-range guns here and preferred to use their artillery to fire on targets their observers could see closer to the line.

The 1/4th Lincolns and their friends, the 1/5th Leicesters, had two small Flemish villages as their rest areas. The first was Dranoutre, which was used only for the first of the three months the North Midland Division held this sector. There was then a change to Locre, just a mile north, for the remaining time in order to conform to the front line sectors being held by the two battalions in those weeks. The Flemish language used by the inhabitants of this area was not permitted to be used on any form of official documents at that time, so the maps used by the British Army contained the French names for all the local towns and most of the villages. So, what the local people called Dranouter, Loker and distant Ieper, appeared on the maps with their French equivalents of Dranoutre, Locre and Ypres. The British used those names in all everyday matters and all records. The ban on the use of Flemish no longer applies, which is why a visitor who now goes looking for Locre, for example, finds Loker instead. This story will use the French names that the First World War soldiers used. Battalions out of the line were billeted, not in the villages, but either in farm buildings or in recently erected hutted camps around the villages. The 1/4th Lincolns seem always to have been in huts throughout their whole time in this area. Facilities were only basic – initially only straw on the floor for sleeping, no heating, cold water washing and an occasional communal bath in the vats of a small brewery in Kemmel. But these were merely the usual hallmarks of active service soldiering.

The battalion transport and cooks were located at a nearby farm and hot food always awaited men returning from their tours of the trenches. The ensuing days were spent resting, drilling, training or on the relentless working parties, but there was some free time. The village cafés were the ritual destinations in the evenings and the town of Bailleul, though over the border in France, was only two miles from Dranoutre. A café and cake shop run by a pretty girl called Tina and her mother was the smart place there, but it was probably reserved for 'Officers Only'. The only serious border controls in operation were those between the Allies and the Germans in No Man's Land. There was little danger. No shells fell. No German aircraft ventured this far over the lines during those months. Zeppelins flew overhead twice, probably en route to England, although one bomb fell harmlessly near Dranoutre. Generals showed their faces occasionally. The Bishop of Pretoria visited Locre one Sunday in May and confirmed several members of the 1/4th Lincolns.

The Lincolns made a rough cricket pitch at Locre and played two challenge matches. The ball and bats were made from willow poles. Private

George Martin, a pre-war Boston Town footballer, sent home the results which were published in the *Lincolnshire Standard*. The 1/5th Lincolns were beaten 40 runs to 25, the 1/5th Leicesters 43 to 16. The Leicesters' team must have been made up from 'rear details' because the main battalion was in the line at the time. For some reason not stated, all the teams contained twelve players. It must have been a bowlers' wicket. Private Martin was a star bowler, taking eight wickets in each match, and only one batsman, listed as 'Lieutenant Hall' reached double figures; he scored 11 runs playing for the 1/4th Lincolns against the Leicesters.

It is believed that this Lieutenant Hall was not actually a Lincolns' officer but was visiting from another battalion as a guest of Captain Staniland. He will play an important part in our story. Arthur Hall was Mrs Staniland's brother. He had introduced his sister to Meaburn Staniland when the latter was visiting Louth and had been best man at their wedding in 1909. When Arthur Hall became a Regular officer before the war, he could not find a vacancy in the Lincolns but was commissioned in the Dorsetshire Regiment. He was now with the 1st Dorsets, in the 5th Division which was holding the southern part of the Ypres Salient sector.

The time spent in Dranoutre and Locre must have been in many ways like a pre-war annual summer camp indefinitely prolonged. And it was summer

Officers of the 1/4 Lincolns 'at rest' in huts, either at Dranoutre or at Locre. Left to right: Lieutenant Drysdale (MO), Lieutenant H. C. Marris (head only), Major Barrell, Lieutenant Colonel Jessop, Lieutenant Gray, Lieutenant Pennell, Major Cooper, Second Lieutenant Newton. Lieutenant Gray, obviously just aroused from sleep, was the officer who took over the Boston Company when Meaburn Stanliland was killed but was then killed himself at the Hohenzollern Redoubt.

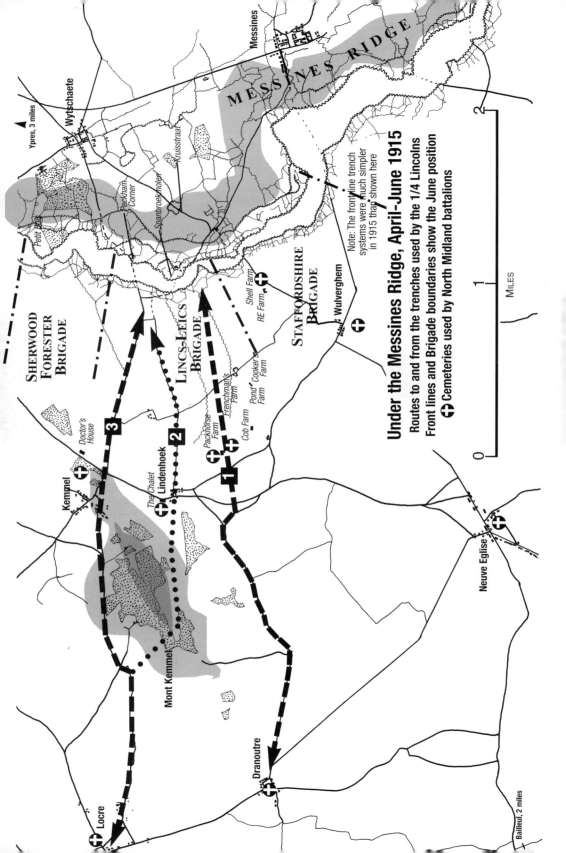

Under the Messines Ridge, April–June 1915

Routes to and from the trenches used by the 1/4 Lincolns
Front lines and Brigade boundaries show the June position
✠ Cemeteries used by North Midland battalions

Note: The front line trench
systems were much simpler
in 1915 that shown here

MESSINES RIDGE

Messines

Wytschaete

Ypres, 3 miles

Peckham Corner

Spanbroekmolen

Kruisstraat

Petit Bois

SHERWOOD
FORESTER
BRIGADE

LINCS-LEICS
BRIGADE

STAFFORDSHIRE
BRIGADE

Wulverghem

Shell Farm
RE Farm

Frenchman's Farm

Pond Cooker Farm
Farm

Cob Farm

Packhorse Farm

Doctor's House

Kemmel

The Chalet
Lindenhoek

Mont Kemmel

Locre

Dranoutre

Neuve Eglise

Bailleul, 2 miles

0   1   2
MILES

The Chalet at Lindenhoek used as HQ by various battalions.

now. The pre-war Boston Territorials were still nearly all together, sharing their firm comradeship.

Dranoutre and Locre were both four miles from the front line. The map on page 30 shows the routes taken by the 1/4th Lincolns and 1/5th Leicesters every time they marched up to or back from the trenches. The map also shows the locations where the battalions established their HQs when their companies were in the line. The Lincolns found their first HQ at Frenchman's Farm was too close to the front, particularly after casualties were suffered from shelling at nearby Pond Farm during that first trench tour. So Cob Farm, half a mile further back, was used for the next three tours. The Lincolns used a slightly damaged building at Lindenhoek called the Chalet during the following three trench tours when the Spanbroekmolen-Peckham Corner trenches were being manned. This pleasant, slightly hilly, part of Flanders was a pre-war holiday area for people from the industrial towns of Belgium and northern France. The Lindenhoek Chalet is believed to have been the holiday home of a factory owner from Lille. Finally, a substantial building known as the Doctor's House on the eastern edge of Kemmel was used twice towards the end of the three-month-long divisional tour on this sector. The building was the home of the local doctor, Dr Alfred Ruypens, a batchelor. Both Lindenhoek Chalet and the Doctor's House would become further permanent British Army names. The Doctor's House was to prove a particularly tragic place for the 1/4th Lincolns.

Trench Action

Even in the least active of trench sectors there was ever-present danger. German snipers, always with the advantage of higher ground, were among the foremost cause of casualties for the North Midland men under the Messines Ridge. Steel helmets had not yet been introduced and most sniper hits were in the head and usually led to instant death. British snipers tried hard to retaliate and there were many sniper duels. My uncle, Sergeant Crick, took part in some of these. He was slightly wounded on one occasion while in the Spanbroekmolen-Peckham Corner trenches when a German opponent hit the top of his trench periscope and smashed the glass, pieces of which flew down the body of the periscope and cut his face. A letter home from one of his friends said that this led 'to a small operation, painful but not dangerous; he was soon back in the trenches'. Shellfire was the other main danger. A common German practice was to batter down a section of the sandbag breastwork in the British line, and then turn machine-gun and rifle fire onto the gap while efforts were being made to repair it. German artillery observers had a great advantage. From positions in or near their front line on the higher ground, they could safely view, not only the British front line just below them, but also all the farms, lanes, tracks and open ground up to two miles away. The British were at a clear disadvantage as their best observation posts were on Mont Kemmel, a mile and a half from the nearest point of the German line.

The Germans made no serious attacks on the line held by the North Midland Division during the whole three months of its tenure of this area. There was a bungled trench raid on the line of the 1/4th Lincolns at Peckham Corner on 13 May. The Germans guessed, correctly, that the British line contained a shaft down to a tunnel leading under the trenches in the German line. They were not to know that the tunnel was not making much progress due to the absence here of any Royal Engineer Tunnelling Companies at this time. After an afternoon of deliberate shelling had broken down the breastwork, the Germans sprayed the resulting gap with machine-gun fire to cover the approach in the evening gloom of a raiding party estimated at forty strong carrying explosive charges to destroy the shaft. After a brisk action the Germans withdrew, leaving one dead Bavarian and two unexploded charges at the bottom of the shaft. Two Lincolns were killed and several wounded. A company of the 1/5th Leicesters had to rush

*Sergeant Albert Preston, Boston-born but serving in the mainly Lincoln 'D'
Company, observing the German lines from a reserve trench cut into an old wheat
field. The other soldiers are probably Lincoln men.*

An unidentified Lincolns marksman using a 'sniperscope' from a front-line trench opposite the Messines Ridge. Note again the sandbagged breastwork, this time with the raised firestep which was manned only at dawn and dusk 'stand to' or if a German attack developed; to stand on it at any other time in daylight risked instant death from a German sniper bullet.

up from the rear and help man the line while the Lincolns repaired the damage to their trench during the night.

The Germans carried out more extensive tunnelling. The 1/5th Lincolns were the victims of the most serious German mine explosion. Part of the battalion was holding a short, isolated section of trench known as E1 Left. It was an evil place, in advance of the main British line and only 30 yards from the German line. A garrison of one officer and twenty men was always posted there. The Leicesters had been raided there just before midnight on 10 May and been temporarily evicted. A counterattack re took the trench, and they found a dead Bavarian officer and a dying Leicesters' company commander, Captain Henry Haylock. The German officer was measured as 6 ft, 3 in. It was said that he had been given the task of leading the raid as punishment for some misdemeanour he had committed, but how that was ascertained is not known. Then, without warning on the afternoon of 20 May, the Germans exploded a large mine under the E1 Left when it was the turn of the 1/5th Lincolns to hold it. Most of the defending party were killed or buried. Frantic efforts to save the buried men took place, but German riflemen took a toll of those rescuers who exposed themselves. Sixteen Lincolns were killed, so too was an officer of the divisional Royal Engineers who was directing the rescue. He was hit just as the recovery work was completed. Two of the dead Lincolns were brothers, Privates Ernest and James Proctor from Scunthorpe, both scoutmasters before the war. The Royal Engineers

officer was Lieutenant Douglas Gosling from Birmingham. The bodies of four of the Lincolns were never recovered and remain entombed in that ground just below the Messines Ridge. This was the worst single incident in the Lincolns-Leicesters Brigade during its three months in this area. A temporary tunnelling company was later formed in the brigade to counter future German efforts, many of its men being former miners from the Leicestershire coalfield. They had several successes, blowing in some German galleries before they reached the British line. Tunnelling was one activity where the lie of the land was advantageous to the British. Being on the lower ground, the British did not have to dig such deep entrance shafts before they could start making level galleries running towards the German trenches.

Violent actions like those described above, however, were rare. Men in the front line had to remain alert, as well as continually maintaining and improving their trenches. They were joined by men from support companies and working parties from the resting battalions at Dranoutre who came up at night to help with such tasks as joining up the isolated stretches of breastworks to make a continuous line, providing a screen of barbed wire in No Man's Land, or the digging of communication trenches. Until the communication trenches, which offered protection from stray shots, were completed, the nightly journeys of ration parties and the exchange of battalions holding the front line every four nights had to take place over open. Two long communication trenches were eventually finished on the Lincolnshire-Leicestershire Brigade sector: they were named Regent Street and Piccadilly. The Sherwood Foresters completed another one from near Kemmel which was called, for some obscure reason, Via Gellia. North of that trench there was only a very exposed approach to the front line known as the Sahara Desert.

There was a steady trickle of casualties – a few dead, more wounded, many sick. The bodies of French and British soldiers killed earlier had sometimes been buried in the base of the thick sandbag breastworks of the front line and were now rotting in the warmer weather. Many of the fields near the line had not been harvested the previous autumn and the stench of rotting vegetables and of dead pigs and cattle was everywhere. When a dud shell fell in an old sugar beet clamp, the men digging for it were driven away by the stench. Lance Corporal Jasper Sharpe wrote home to Boston to report his first lice infestation on 6 May. Two men from a North Staffordshire battalion gave themselves self-inflicted wounds to escape conditions that they felt they could no longer face. All these casualties were the usual steady cost of attrition for units in even the quietest of sectors.

One interesting diversion came at the end of May with the arrival in the divisional sector of some battalions from the 14th (Light) Division, one of the first New Army divisions to proceed to the Western Front. Just as their hosts had been helped by battalions of the 4th Division two months earlier, platoons from the 7th Rifle Brigade and the 11th Durham Light Infantry were attached to the 1/4th Lincolns and 1/5th Leicesters for their introduction to trench conditions. There was some tension. The New Army units considered themselves part of the Regular Army and, though their men were almost entirely wartime volunteers, believed their training and discipline were superior to that of Territorials. Another of Lance Corporal Sharpe's letters home – he was a prolific correspondent – says, 'They consider themselves far ahead of mere Terriers. It rather knocks them to have to be with us at all, and of course we are taking the opportunity to get as much fun out of it as possible. They are decent chaps, but unfortunately suffering from a slight touch of swelled head. I really believe they consider these hostilities will soon cease now that they have come out. They have said nearly as much'. The attitude of one of the visiting 14th Division's platoon commanders was shaken when his sergeant reported, in front of the 1/5th Leicesters, that a man had been wounded by an accidental rifle discharge. However, having carried a Maxim machine-gun under each arm and a tripod over one shoulder a Durham Light Infantry machine-gun officer from the new division, also attached to the Leicesters, was praised both for his bravery and for his strength in rushing to the help of the Leicesters when a small mine exploded under their trench.

The two 14th Division battalions suffered three fatal casualties during their period of instruction. Nineteen-year-old Rifleman Matthew North of the Rifle Brigade, from Old Alresford in Hampshire, who was killed on 31 May, may have been the division's first fatal casualty on active service. The other two dead were Durham men.

Killed in Action

A battalion in an inexperienced division like the North Midland could expect to suffer an average of two or three men killed during each four-day tour of trench duty on a sector such as the one being held under the Messines Ridge during those first three months. But the death of each man was a tragedy that brought sadness to a family somewhere at home, and it also brought about the steady weakening of the bonds of comradeship among those Territorials who had served and trained together before the war.

The 1/4th Lincolns got off to a bad start in their first spell of front line duty. Two men were killed – both from the Stamford Company on 10 and 11 April, the first two days in the trenches. They were Privates Harry Mason from Little Bytham and Charles Baker from Stamford. Two days later, on the last day of the tour, a German artillery observer must have spotted movement at the support position at Pond Farm, three-quarters of a mile behind the front line. Lieutenant Charles Ellwood, a farmer from Mareham-le-Fen, was at another farm nearby and, in a letter to his mother written as the incident took place, describes what happened.

Dear Mother,

I am writing this during our 4 days spell in the trenches. I am not actually in the trenches, but in a battered house 500 or 600 yards behind. We are like owls and don't come out until dark. The Germans think the farm is not occupied and if we showed ourselves in the daytime they would shell it to bits at once...

I have just been up into the roof watching the shells burst all around. They have just put two on a farm 150 yards further back where we have

100 men. They have just run out and taken cover in some old dugouts. One shell burst on the roof and we have just heard has killed one of our officers and some men. They are still shelling the farm but are wasting their ammunition as all our men have cleared out.

Ellwood's figure of '100 men' at the shelled farm was an unintentional overestimate. The troops were from a Spalding platoon. Two men, including the officer, were killed and seven men were wounded, one of whom died later. The dead officer was Second Lieutenant Geoffrey Staniland, the brother of Captain Meaburn Staniland, the Boston Company commander. The Spalding soldier killed was Private Frank Bridges. Geoffrey Staniland's front line career had lasted less than four days. The usual tactful, but probably untruthful, letter was sent to his home in Louth: 'He fell dead, struck through the heart.' That early death of Geoffrey Staniland was the first of an unusually high proportion of officer casualties which would be suffered by the 1/4th Lincolns and the start of a tragic process for the Staniland family which would extend over many years.

Five men died on that first trench tour. The next three tours would be less costly, with six men killed. One was another officer, Second Lieutenant Wilfred Hirst, a Yorkshireman from Rotherham. Another letter from Lieutenant Ellwood describes Hirst's death:

We lost another officer last night. He was in charge of a party who were bringing our rations and he was shot through the head by a stray bullet about 300 yards behind our trench. The Germans were firing rather heavily at us at that time and a large number of the bullets go over our parapet and land all over the country.

The pre-war Boston Company suffered its first fatal casualties when Privates James Chamberlain of Witham Street and Ernest Dallywaters of Minden Terrace, Hospital Lane, were killed during the third spell in the line. Chamberlain was aged nineteen, Dallywaters only eighteen. Letters from friends stated that both men were victims of German snipers. Chamberlain must have been a careful fellow; thirty francs in notes were found in his wallet and returned home by Major Cooper. It may have been at this time that another Boston man was fatally wounded. He was Private John Thompson, a former Boston Grammar School boy whose father owned a flour milling business in Spilsby Road. A letter that has survived showed how, on the outbreak of war, this young man had beseeched his father for permission to volunteer for overseas service and not be left behind with those 'who had simply joined the Territorials so that they could walk about in the street in uniform'. He was hit in the head while helping to carry a wounded man on a stretcher and evacuated to England where he had died in a military hospital at Sheffield. He was buried in the churchyard of Holy Trinity, directly opposite his home at 43 Spilsby Road. There would be no further deaths of Boston men during the three months of service on this sector.*

The most costly trench tour for the 1/4th Lincolns was the fifth, which for some unrecorded reason lasted for six days instead of the normal four. It was during this tour that the Germans carried out a trench raid on the line at Peckham Corner on 13 May. Seven men were killed or later died of wounds received on that tour. A further casualty at that time was Lieutenant Geoffrey Marris (the younger of the two Marris officer brothers) who was buried alive by a shell and so concussed that he was evacuated, first to the large convent at Locre, which was being used by one of the division's medical units, and then back to England. However he would return to the front again.

The remaining four trench tours brought the deaths of just eight more of the battalion's men. One was another officer, Lieutenant Charles Ellwood, whose earlier letters have been so helpful. He had been a long-serving pre-war member of the now dispersed pre-war Horncastle Company. He was another sniper victim, shot through the left eye. The battalion lost the services of two company commanders at this time, one promoted to be second in command of the 1/4th Leicesters, the other becoming ill and returning to England.

The biggest shock to the battalion, however, did not come as a result of action in the trenches. The gradual leftward allocation to battalions of front line trenches meant that new locations had to be found in the immediate rear for the headquarters of battalions when their companies were in the line. Early in June, the 1/4th Lincolns and the 1/5th Leicesters stopped using Lindenhoek Chalet and had to start using the building on the forward edge of Kemmel village known as the 'Doctor's House'. The Leicesters were the first to use it. On 4

The 'Doctor's House' at Kemmel, photographed by an officer of the 1/7th Sherwood Foresters when his battalion was using it as HQ before the Leicesters and Lincolns took over.

*The details of Private Thompson's death, and of many other Boston men, are taken from *A Town Remembers, Those Commemorated on The Boston War Memorial, Volume 1 – The First World War* by Dr William M. Hunt.

June, while the Lincolns were resting at Locre, Lieutenant Colonel Jessop, the Lincolns' commanding officer, and his two majors, Oliver Cooper and Gilbert Barrell, went forward on horseback to meet Lieutenant Colonel C. H. Jones of the Leicesters to view the new HQ the Lincolns would soon be using.

Kemmel was not a healthy place, three Belgian children having been killed by shellfire in the village square a week earlier. The two majors were taken to see the new trenches. The two colonels chatted. Two soldiers of the Leicesters held the three horses. The Germans on Messines Ridge a mile and a half away probably saw the horses. Shells fell with perfect accuracy. Lieutenant Colonel Jessop was killed, as were the two Leicester soldiers and the horses they were holding. Lieutenant Colonel Jones was wounded in three places. He had to be evacuated to England but would return to his command later. The death of Lieutenant Colonel Jessop caused the

Lieutenant Colonel Jessop, originally a Medical Officer, then OC of the Horncastle Company in the Territorials, finally Battalion Commander of the 1/4th Lincolns. He wears the ribbon of the 1911 Coronation Medal.

Leicesters to stay an extra two days in the trenches. Major Barrell, before the war a wine merchant from Spalding, became the new commanding officer of the Lincolns. This setback was an example of the Territorials' failure to adapt quickly to the realities of service at the front – three officers going into an area under German observation on horseback in broad daylight! It was hard luck on the two Leicester soldiers killed while holding the horses.

Burying The Dead

There are over 150 British military cemeteries in the part of Belgium in which the British presence was so intensive for four years in the First World War. They range in size between the impressively huge, but somewhat impersonal, post-war concentration cemeteries like Tyne Cot, to the numerous small ones which the British, so emotionally moved by the scale of wartime sacrifice, could not bring themselves to close after the war. The Imperial War Graves Commission was charged with the task of making permanent as many of the smaller ones as could practicably be maintained. Fortunately for today's visitors, the Commonwealth War Graves Commission still maintains these for our study and pilgrimage tours.

The fierce fighting in 1914, when the Germans had pushed the BEF back almost to the gates of Ypres and, on this sector, to the edge of the Messines Ridge, had not allowed the British to bury their dead in a systematic manner. Some units had seen it as a matter of honour at that time to carry out of battle the bodies of their dead officers if possible and bury them in the nearest available village churchyard or town cemetery. Good examples of such graves can be found in the churchyard at Zillebeke and just inside the side gate of Ypres Town Cemetery, on the left hand side of the road out to Hooge and Menin. (Use a gap in the nearby hedge if the gate is locked.) The static conditions of winter had resulted in fewer casualties and more opportunity for orderly burials, but the available spaces in the civilian cemeteries, particularly in the village churchyards, soon filled up and the new concept of making purely military cemeteries in open ground had to be introduced, particularly in areas close to the front line.

It was found convenient to establish these new burial grounds in fields close to where battalions had their headquarters when their companies were occupying front line trenches. The aid post of a battalion medical officer as well as the entrance to a communication trench leading to the front line were usually nearby. The bodies of men killed in the trenches and carried out at night, and of those dying at the aid post, could thus be buried at a convenient place. There are many such cemeteries just behind the trench systems on sectors of the Western Front where conditions were static for long periods. I call them 'comrades' cemeteries' because the dead were usually buried by men of their own units. When it arrived for its first spell of active service on this front the North Midland Division was particularly active in this respect.

In the area to which the Lincolnshire-Leicestershire Brigade came in early April 1915, two such cemeteries were immediately established at places about a mile and a half behind the front line. (The cemeteries referred to in this section are shown on Map One, on page 30. A description of them as they appear today will be provided towards the end of the book). The 1/4th Lincolns and the 1/5th Leicesters who shared the front line duty in the north of the brigade sector started a cemetery at Packhorse Farm and the 1/5th Lincolns and 1/4th Leicesters started their cemetery near a roadside shrine only a short distance southward down the same lane. It became known as Packhorse Farm Shrine Cemetery.

After the first three trench tours in April, however, the battalions had to start holding trenches slightly further north. The 1/4th Lincolns and 1/5th Leicesters moved their billets from Dranoutre to Locre and started using Lindenhoek Chalet as their HQ when in the trenches. The departing Sherwood Foresters had started making a small cemetery at Lindenhoek Chalet, burying fifteen men of their 1/5th and 1/7th Battalions there. The incoming Lincolns and Leicesters used the same field for the remainder of their time in this area, through the months of May and June. When the North Midland Division left for a new sector at the end of June, the 1/4th Lincolns and 1/5th Leicesters left behind in those little field cemeteries the graves of thirty-two men – seven and nine respectively at Packhorse Farm and eight for each battalion at Lindenhoek Chalet. The other two battalions in the brigade, the 1/5th Lincolns and 1/4th Leicesters, continued to use their first cemetery at Packhorse Farm Shrine throughout the entire three months, leaving the graves of twenty-six Lincolns and twenty-seven Leicesters there.

Also buried among the Lincolns at Packhorse Farm Shrine are two other North Midland Division casualties, one Royal Engineer and a man from the Royal Army Medical Corps. In addition and buried among the Leicesters, are three soldiers of the 14th (Light) Division killed during their period of trench acclimatization.

Not all the dead were buried in those cemeteries. One man from the 1/4th Lincolns and four from the 1/5th Lincolns whose bodies were buried by German mine explosions are commemorated on the Memorial to the Missing at the Menin Gate at Ypres. Men who died of wounds after leaving the trenches – seven from the 1/4th Lincolns and three from the 1/5th – are buried elsewhere, either at the nearest casualty clearing station just over the French border at Bailleul, at base hospitals on the French coast, or in England. The locations of the graves of the 'died of wounds' for the Leicester battalions and the other brigades have not been researched.

The other brigades in the division broadly used a similar system for burying their dead. In the Staffordshire Brigade area, the village of Wulverghem (now Wulvergem) was only a mile behind the front line. A few men from battalions in the brigade were buried in the village churchyard in early May, but this practice soon ceased, probably because the churchyard became full. The 1/5th and 1/6th South Staffords then used a small cemetery recently opened near a roadside inn called St Quentin Cabaret just outside the village and the two North Staffords battalions moved to a similar small existing cemetery at R. E. Farm for their burials, even though this was less than half a mile behind the front line. However the Germans seem to have respected all of the cemeteries and they were not deliberately shelled. The four

The remains of a British soldier found in the Messines Ridge area in 1959.

battalions of the Sherwood Forester Brigade had a simpler system. Six officers and 107 other ranks killed in their trenches were buried in the grounds of Kemmel Chateau (this is in addition to the fifteen graves they left at Lindenhoek Chalet) and thirteen Sherwood Foresters who died of wounds were buried in Locre churchyard. As Locre was shielded from German observation by Mont Kemmel, various units could be located there in reasonable safety.

However the little cemeteries made by the 1/4th Lincolns at Packhorse Farm and Lindenhoek Chalet did not contain the graves of any of its four officers killed in those three months. When the battalion first marched into Dranoutre on 6 April, they found the usual large church and surrounding churchyard common to Flemish villages. In nearly every available space were the graves of eighty-one British soldiers of all ranks buried since November 1914. When Second Lieutenant Geoffrey Staniland and the Spalding soldier, Private Bridges, were killed by shrapnel at Pond Farm, the body of Private Bridges was left at Packhorse Farm for burial but that of Second Lieutenant Staniland was brought back a further two and a half miles to Dranoutre. The practice of bringing the bodies of its dead officers from the battlefield to be buried in civilian cemeteries was going out of use. Nearly every other unit in the North Midland Division buried all their ranks together in the new field cemeteries. Only a narrow piece of ground alongside a boundary wall remained in Dranoutre churchyard. It was just wide enough and Geoffrey Staniland was buried at one end of that strip. Lance Corporal William Kent, the monumental mason from Boston and a friend of the Staniland family, probably helped prepare the grave and later made a marker and a small concrete surround for it. When Second Lieutenant Hirst was killed on 22 April, his body was

The first two officers' graves in the strip of ground at the side of Dranoutre churchyard. The grave of Second Lieutenant Geoffrey Staniland has two crosses, the larger one probably made by the 1/4 Lincolns, the smaller one, with more enduring metal tags, by an official graves registration unit. The second grave is that of Second Lieutenant Hirst. The photograph must have been taken between 22 April and 20 May 1915, when an RE officer Lieutenant Gosling, would be buried. The concrete surrounds might have been made by Lance Corporal Kent, the Boston monumental mason.

brought to be buried just behind Geoffrey Staniland.

The Lincolns then left Dranoutre and, when not in the trenches, Locre, a mile and a half further north, became its billeting village. The battalion would spend twice as much time at Locre than at Dranoutre and there was plenty of space in Locre churchyard for burials. That did not matter. The Lincolns obviously felt an affinity with the village they had occupied when coming into the line for the first time and when Lieutenant Ellwood was killed on 2 June and Lieutenant Colonel Jessop two days later, their bodies were taken to Dranoutre. A third officer's grave had appeared there, that of Lieutenant Gosling, the Royal Engineers officer killed in the rescue work after the Germans exploded a mine under the trench of the 1/5th Lincolns on 20 May. Ellwood and Jessop became the fourth and fifth graves in that line. Lieutenant Colonel Jessop's funeral, on the afternoon of 5 June, was a major event, attended by the divisional commander, Major General Hon. E. J. Montagu-Stuart-Wortley, many other high ranking officers and a large number of the Lincoln Territorials.

That is how the 1/4th Lincolns buried their officers, head to toe in that narrow space on the edge of the churchyard at Dranoutre. It will be shown later that there was a direct link between those events and the naming of a house built in Boston more than ten years afterwards.

Marching Orders

The 1/4th Lincolns were relieved from a routine tour of duty in the trenches during the night of 21 June, the shortest night of the year. The incoming troops were not, however, their old friends of the 1/5th Leicesters; both battalions were now finished with this sector. The new battalion was the 1/9th Durham Light Infantry, part of the battered Territorial Northumbrian Division whose battalions had suffered so severely when rushed in piecemeal to save the line following the German gas attack at Ypres. By coincidence, the Lincolns had been giving trench instruction only two days earlier to New Army men of the 10th Durhams, part of the 14th (Light) Division. The remnants of the Northumbrian Division were now to recuperate on this quiet sector, while the North Midland Division was to move north to the main Ypres Salient. Another division to have suffered badly at Ypres, the 28th Regular, also came down for a rest here. The two divisions could only muster sufficient strength to take over this one normal divisional frontage from the North Midland Division. Fortunately the fighting at Ypres had died down, so once again it would be trench-holding duty for the North Midland on a relatively settled sector, though not as quiet as the one they were just leaving.

The division had been able to spend three months without being involved in serious action. Its men had become hardened to active service conditions and had also carried out much valuable work, not only holding their trenches safely but, by much hard labour, considerably strengthening the defences. The cost in casualties had not been heavy. Fatal casualties in the twelve infantry battalions during their earlier visits to the trenches for instruction and then the three months of trench holding numbered twenty-seven officers and 373 other ranks. The numbers of men evacuated wounded or sick was approximately three times that of the dead. Total infantry casualties in the division were thus about 1,600, about twenty per day, or about 14 per cent of the original infantry strength. Among the casualties evacuated as sick were several senior NCOs, warrant officers, captains, majors, two battalion commanders and one brigade commander who, despite his protests had found conditions so rigorous that his health had collapsed and he had been returned home. A second brigade commander would follow in August. (The number of fatal casualties can be ascertained with near certainty from the official publications *Officers Died in the Great War and Soldiers Died in the Great War.* There is no easily accessible source for wounds and sickness, but scattered references in various battalion histories published after the war indicate that the approximate one-to-three ratio of killed to other casualties for the North Midland battalions in these months is valid. The losses of other units in the division have not been researched; they were light in comparison and this study is restricted to the infantry battalions.)

The unit which suffered the highest number of fatal casualties was the 1/8th Sherwood Foresters, the battalion from the country towns of Nottinghamshire. Its dead numbered four officers and fifty-nine other ranks, with a high proportion of sentries hit in the head by sniper bullets and fourteen men killed in one day in April by a prolonged trench-mortar bombardment. The most fortunate battalion was the 1/7th Sherwood Foresters, the Nottingham City battalion, with one officer and seventeen other ranks killed. The 1/4th Lincolns had lost four officers and twenty-four other ranks killed, a below average figure for the division, but it was the only battalion to have had its commanding officer killed.

The North Midland Division had indeed been fortunate. While the division had been losing dead counted in a few hundred over a period of three months, thousands of British and Canadians had been killed stemming the German offensive in front of Ypres less than ten miles to the north. A visible reminder of the cost of that fighting had been the passage through the rear of the divisional area of a stream of motor ambulances carrying gas victims and wounded for two days and nights to the casualty clearing station at Bailleul. On arrival at Bailleul, the waiting casualties were rumoured to have filled half of the town square. Other British divisions had suffered heavily in attacks at Aubers Ridge and Festubert twenty miles to the south and the French had shed massive amounts of blood at the Lorette Spur and on Vimy Ridge, a further ten miles distant.

The 1/4th Lincolns and the 1/5th Leicesters, and probably other battalions, were visited on 22 June by Lieutenant General Sir Charles Fergusson, the commander of II Corps. He thanked the units for their service under his command and wished them well for the future. The two battalions marched out of Locre for the last time that evening, heading north. It was just a three mile march, but to an unfamiliar area.

The hamlet of Ouderdom was their destination. There were few farms and a shortage of hutted camps. The battalions had to settle in fields, the soldiers making three-man bivouacs with groundsheets and any sticks or poles they could find. The division was given one week of 'rest' before going into trenches on its new sector. For the 1/4th Lincolns there were two days of 'interior economy', that army phrase which was still current when I did my National Service in the 1950s – arranging accommodation, cleaning personal equipment for inspection and resting when possible. Next came two days of route marches, seven miles each day, the exact distance to the new trenches, followed by three days of mixed digging of a reserve line and more route marching.

A draft of eighty-nine reinforcements arrived for the battalion during that week. Some were men who had recovered from wounds or sickness but most were from the 2/4th Lincolns, the Second Line battalion in England that was training the wartime Territorial volunteers. They were good, willing men, nearly all from South Lincolnshire, and they brought a welcome renewal and reinvigoration of the local Territorial spirit to the battalion. A useful

Part of the 1/4th Lincolns in bivouacs, probably at Ouderdom soon after the battalion was transferred to the Ypres Salient sector at the end of June 1915.

note in the War Diary records the new strength as twenty-six officers and 898 other ranks with which the battalion must tackle its next task. This was still about five officers and a hundred men below the proper war establishment.

A month earlier the War Office had finally allocated divisional numbers to the Territorial divisions. The thirty-six divisions of Kitchener's 'New Army' were numbered after the Regulars with the last formed of the new divisions becoming the 41st. Despite the fact that five Territorial divisions had been in action on the Western Front before the first of the new armies had arrived, when they followed on from the 41st, the Territorial divisions were at last formally admitted to the acknowledged ranks of the British Army. The 42nd to 45th Divisions were those which left England early to replace the Regulars in garrisons along the sea route to India, Australia and New Zealand, and in India itself. The first division to go to the Western Front, our North Midland Division, came next with the full title of 46th (1st North Midland) Division; we can call it the 46th Division, although I still find myself wanting to use 'the North Midland Division' more often. The brigades in the division were also numbered with this result:

> Staffordshire Brigade .... 137 Brigade
> Lincolnshire-Leicestershire Brigade .... 138 Brigade
> Sherwood Forester Brigade .... 139 Brigade

The unfortunate Northumbrian Division which had just taken over the 46th Division's sector became the 50th Division. The other pre-war Territorial divisions which arrived on the Western Front in 1915 were the 47th (2nd London), 48th (South Midland), 49th (West Riding) and 51st (Highland). The 52nd (Lowland), 53rd (Welsh) and 54th (East Anglian) Divisions all went to Gallipoli. The remaining two pre-war divisions had sent so many battalions out individually to support the BEF in 1914 that they could not reform until 1916 when they became the 55th (West Lancashire) and 56th (1st London) Divisions. Their first actions as complete divisions were to come in the Battle of the Somme.

On the evening of 28 June, the 1/4th Lincolns marched off from Ouderdom to start taking over trenches in the new divisional sector and to commence the next phase of their war service.

PART THREE

The Ypres Salient

The New Divisional Sector

The 46th Division now formed part of Lieutenant General Sir Edmund Allenby's V Corps in General Sir Herbert Plumer's Second Army which bore the heavy responsibility of defending the Ypres Salient. V Corps held the southern part of the salient. The 46th Division would be taking over the line at its most easterly point and then about a third of the way down the southern face, generally facing south-east, with a total frontage of just over two miles. The division was replacing the weakened 50th (Northumbrian) Division and also parts of the line of the 3rd Division on the left and the 5th Division on the right. So, what was by Western Front standards a strong, fresh division was to replace a battered Territorial division and also relieve two Regular divisions, weakened by constant fighting since the outbreak of war, of parts of their front line responsibilities.

The takeover was a gradual one and had to be carefully arranged because many of the North Midland Division battalions could not leave their old sectors until replaced by the Northumbrians. The Sherwood Forester Brigade came in first, in the north of the new sector, followed by the Lincolnshire-Leicestershire Brigade in the centre, with the Staffordshire Brigade coming in last in the south. This brigade disposition was the same as in the earlier trench tour. The northernmost part of the new sector was just below the infamous Menin Road near the village of Hooge (now Hoge). For the next mile and a half, the opposing lines ran through or between a series of what had been dense woods. These still retained a certain proportion of growth but would steadily be reduced to the barren stumplands shown in photographs taken later in the war. From north to south, the line ran through or by Zouave, Sanctuary and Armagh Woods, with the smaller Maple Copse and Fosse Wood all about half a mile behind the front line. This part of the divisional area was in complete contrast to that of its earlier service. Although the ground held by the Germans was slightly higher than that of the British, the woods denied the Germans the superb observation they had enjoyed from the Messines Ridge.

There were three small hills among these woods, the possession of which would give whoever held them an obvious local advantage. The first two, coming down from the north, were Hill 62 – also known both as Tor Top – at the southern end of Sanctuary Wood which was in British hands, and Hill

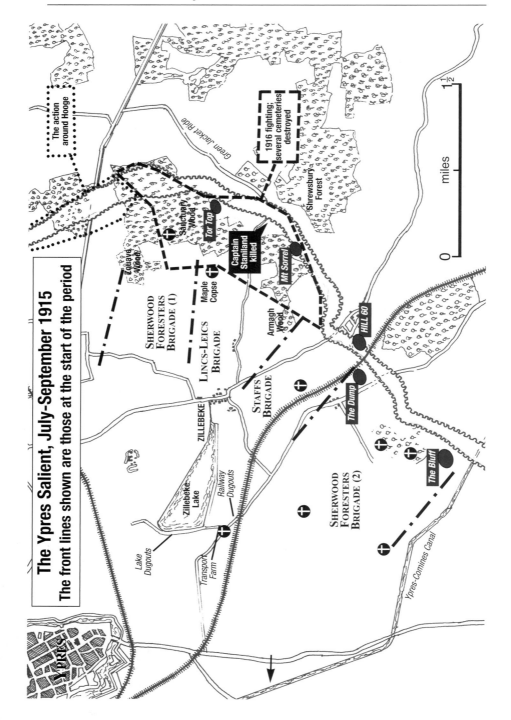

The Ypres Salient, July–September 1915
The front lines shown are those at the start of the period

59 on the edge of Armagh Wood; its crest was in No Man's Land. The 1/5th Leicesters christened Hill 59 'Mountsorrel' on their arrival there, after the village near Leicester which was the home of their commanding officer, Lieutenant Colonel C. H. Jones. Army maps, however, would split the new name into two parts, hence the Mount Sorrel many of us know. One of the two Leicester battalions may also have named a local communication trench 'Fosse Way', after the old Roman road running through their county, and Fosse Wood (sometimes called Square Wood.)

A little further south was the evil Hill 60, not a natural feature but the soil dug from a nearby railway cutting. Hill 60 was only fifty feet above the surrounding ground but was important because German possession of it gave them clear observation all the way to Ypres. Initially held by the 5th Division, a fierce local battle in April had left the Germans holding the top of the hill and the 5th Division only on the lower slope a few yards away and counting the cost of a 100 officers and 3,000 men killed or wounded in the recent fighting. Now it would be the infantry of the North Midland Division – the 1/5th North and 1/6th South Staffords for most of the next few weeks – as well as the divisional artillerymen in the rear, who would become vulnerable to the German field of observation from the crest of the hill.

Most of the front-line positions were comparatively new, the recent Second Battle of Ypres having brought the Germans to this area only two months earlier. But the front line was again mostly on low ground so that 'trenches' were again the built-up breastworks made up of thousands of earth-filled sandbags. The line was a continuous one, however, and there

Hill 60 and The Dump in 1915.

Hill 60. A German photograph of what is described as a communication trench to their position on that battle-torn ground.

was also a degree of defence in depth, with good support trenches and strong-points, and also the new concept for the incoming battalions of 'brigade reserve' positions. These consisted of extensive groups of dugouts in embankments capable of holding half a battalion or more of troops about a mile behind the front line, safer than a frontline trench but still within range of enemy shelling. The presence of these brigade reserves arose from the fact that the outskirts of Ypres were only two miles from the front line. It was essential to have reserves close at hand in case of a further German offensive rather than back at the billeting areas such as Ouderdom, seven miles in the rear. Whereas Dranoutre and Locre had been only half that distance from the front. The billeting areas could not be closer because of the geographical reality of holding a salient which protruded into the German lines, rather than holding trenches facing a German bulge into the British lines as at the Messines Ridge. In the British-held area opposite the Messines Ridge, the space available in the British rear radiated out in a fan-shaped arc with ample space for artillery, other support positions and billets within reasonable distance of the line. The ground behind the Ypres Salient was more compressed, like the spokes of a bicycle wheel converging on the hub. All the requirements of war immediately behind the Ypres Salient were perpetually in a cramped and congested area and billeting areas were relegated to the rear.

This, then, was the locality in which the now more experienced – though not yet tempered in battle – North Midland Division would serve the next three months. The ground in front of Ypres had seen the most desperate fighting for the BEF in 1914 and in the earlier part of 1915. No one knew that the Salient had just commenced a two-year period in which there would be no battle. But it would always be an area of menace. Besides the daily hazards of holding the front line trenches in an active sector, there was also the likelihood of vicious local flare-up.

Into the Trenches Again

The 1/4th Lincolns, under the command of the newly promoted Lieutenant Colonel Barrell, set out from Ouderdom for the seven-mile journey to their new front line area on the afternoon of 29 June. The first part of the route they probably took was along a series of tracks in open country, passing on right and left the new sights of numerous supply, transport and medical units, then artillery and reserve infantry positions nearer the line; this

The Zillebeke Lake Dugouts. The steel helmets worn by the troops in the photograph show that it was taken after the period when the North Midland battalions used the dugouts as shelters while in brigade reserve.

The village of Zillebeke.

activity being in contrast to the quieter area they had left behind on their earlier sector. They marched almost to the edge of that famous city of Ypres they had heard so much about, passing through Kruisstraat where the elegant White Chateau remained untouched by shellfire. It was being variously rumoured that the Germans were sparing it because the peacetime owner had been a German, or because the Germans optimistically expected to use it themselves after their next advance. Then the way was over the Ypres-Comines Canal at Bridge 14, a wartime structure built to provide access to the front, and soon across the Ypres-Lille road just north of the road junction which earlier British soldiers had christened Shrapnel Corner. Then it was onwards along the north side of Zillebeke Lake, followed by a dash through the ruined village of Zillebeke because the Germans had a machine-gun on Hill 60 which often sent a burst of fire into the village, a good example of the tactical advantage the Germans had gained when they captured the hill in April. Finally, in late evening, the battalion reached its destination – the little wood half a mile behind the front called Maple Copse. Because the trees of the large Sanctuary Wood ahead and those in Maple Copse itself shielded the marching platoons from German observation, the entire journey had been made in daylight and without

recourse to the tiresome use of communication trenches.

The Lincolns were not due to go into the front line that night but were dispersed into dugouts and shelters of various kinds in Maple Copse and just inside Sanctuary Wood. The ground was on a slight downward slope away from the front line, so all stray shots or bursts of machine-gun fire passed above them, often clipping the upper branches of trees overhead. Many shells fell but no fatal casualties were suffered during the twenty-four hours the Lincolns spent in that wooded area. The battalion went into the front line further inside Sanctuary Wood the next night. The battalion being relieved was none other than the 1st Battalion of their own county regiment serving with the 3rd Division; Lincolnshire Territorials taking over from Lincolnshire Regulars the responsibility of holding this part of the notorious Ypres Salient. The actual front line trenches taken over were known as B4 to B7, with three companies in the actual front line trenches and one in support. Captain Staniland led his 'A' Company into the right-hand front line trench, B4.

That first tour of trench duty lasted six days. No major event took place, but two men – Privates George Mountcastle from Lincoln and Fred Maxwell from Spalding – were killed, and Private Walter Smith from Lincoln later died of wounds. Among the wounded was Captain William

Sanctuary Wood. A strong-point near the front line in the wood in early July 1915, just before the North Midland battalions took over this sector. Note the mostly undamaged trees... and the empty rum jar. The troops were men of the Honourable Artillery Company which, despite its title, was a prestigious pre-war London Territorial infantry battalion that had been sent out in late 1914 to reinforce the hard-pressed Regular 3rd Division. IWM Q49382

Johnson, believed to have been the commander of the Stamford Company, but he would soon recover and be back with his men. The Lincolns were relieved in the early morning hours of 6 July. The incoming battalion was the 1/6th North Staffords who were arriving for their first visit to the Salient trenches. This would not be their regular place in the divisional sector but was the result of the complicated takeover by the North Midland Division of trenches previously held by parts of three other divisions. The Lincolns went back to Ouderdom for six days, a 'rest period' marked by the sudden arrival one day of four heavy shells which wounded one man, and the despatch of a large all-day working party of 420 men sent to dig a reserve line at Kruisstraat.

The location for the next trench tour for the Lincolns was again the result of the complicated divisional takeover of its new sector. Six days were to be spent in the trenches on the lower slope of Hill 60; the battalion being relieved was the 1st Bedfords of the 5th Division. Hill 60 lived up to its reputation and five men were killed – four from Lincoln and the first fatal Boston Company casualty on the Salient, Corporal Charles Burchnall. He was from Freiston and had worked in Boston for Hutsons the ironmongers.

That costly tour ended on the night of 18 July, with the Lincolns again going all the way back to Ouderdom for a further six days of rest and working parties. Compared to what was to come, it had been a relatively easy twenty-five days' introduction to the new sector.

It is not my intention to catalogue every trench tour of the 1/4th Lincolns; suffice at this stage to say that the next two and a half months would be spent in and out of the front line. However, these tours were always in trenches in the southern part of Sanctuary Wood or those just in front of Armagh Wood. This area would become the regular responsibility of the Lincolnshire-Leicestershire Brigade. The 1/4th Lincolns alternated regularly with the 1/5th Leicesters, their old partners from the days and nights spent in the trenches under the Messines Ridge.

The routine that became established for the three months to be spent on the Ypres Salient was based on a twenty-four day cycle. Battalions served six days and nights in the front line, then went back to one of the brigade reserve positions for six days, returned to the trenches for another six-day tour, and then finally back to Ouderdom for six days. Battalions would thus have only a quarter, rather half of the time they had enjoyed in the Messines Ridge sector, in the rear rest area. Three brigade reserve positions would be used by the 1/4th Lincolns. Behind Zillebeke was the large lake of the same name. The western end of the lake had a twenty-foot high bank in the safe side of which was a series of shelters – the Zillebeke Dugouts. Close by there was a railway embankment with a similar series of shelters dug into it – the Railway Embankment Dugouts. The third reserve position used was in the

Poperinghe market place. The tram route commenced at Poperinghe Station.

cellars of a former Belgian Army barracks in Ypres, but the 1/4th Lincolns only used these once. Each location could house troops in reasonable safety but the dugouts, particularly those in the railway embankment, were not completely shell-proof and there were few amenities for troops who might be called to rush into action at any time.

Nor was the rest area at Ouderdom ideal. Unlike homely Dranoutre, Locre and Kemmel and the attractive countryside behind the trenches in the former sector Ouderdom was a small place set in a flat, featureless landscape, with few facilities. It required a long march to and from the trenches. The 1/5th Leicesters once marched the full distance back from a trench tour in the rain, over muddy tracks, and had 150 men reporting sick on arrival. Even as far back as Ouderdom, a long-range German gun known as 'Silent Percy' could land an unexpected blow and although the Lincolns reported no fatal casualties, trenches had to be dug alongside the huts. These

The La Poupée *at Poperinghe probably photographed before the arrival of British troops when it was a combined clothes shop and hotel. It was converted to the famous wartime café.*

problems, together with parades and inspections and the relentless calls for working parties, added up to precious little real 'rest'.

There were some distractions. Ouderdom was only three miles from Poperinghe (now Poperinge) and visits to that almost intact and much loved town could be made. The 'all ranks' soldiers' club at Talbot House had not yet been established; Lieutenant Gilbert Talbot, in whose memory it would be named by the Reverend 'Tubby'

The new café on the site of the La Poupée *at Poperinghe. The* L'Esperance *next door translates as The Hope and was known to British troops as "Wot 'opes". The diamond shaped plaque on the left-hand building provides a description of the wartime history of the buildings.*

11
A LA FABRIQUE,
LA POUPÉE, WHAT 'OPES?

DEZE GEVEL MET HET CAFÉ "A LA
FABRIQUE" IS ÉÉN VAN DE WEINIGE DIE
NIET VERANDERD IS DOOR DE OORLOG.
BIJ DE SOLDATEN HET CAFÉ DE L'ESPERANCE
(NR 17), BEKEND ALS "WHAT 'OPE?" WAT VOOR
HOOP? IN HET HUIS NR 16), WAS "A LA POUPÉE"
GEVESTIGD, HET FAVORIETE RESTAURANT VAN POPERINGE
HET GEHEIM VAN LA POUPÉE? DE GASTVRIJHEID VAN MADAME, EN DE JEUGD
VAN HAAR 3 DOCHTERS. IN HET GOEDE "GINGER", EEN VROEGRIJP KIND VAN
13-15, WAS DE OOGAPPEL VAN VEEL KLANTEN. HET IS OPVALLEND DAT ZE IN VRIJWEL ELK DAG-
BOEK VOORKOMT VAN DE OFFICIEREN DIE EEN POOSJE DE BUURT VAN POP GELEGERD WAREN.

THE FACADE OF THE "A LA FABRIQUE" CAFÉ IS ONE OF THE VERY FEW NOT TO HAVE BEEN AFFECTED BY
THE WAR OR BEEN CHANGED SINCE THEN. TO THE SOLDIERS THE "CAFÉ DE L'ESPERANCE" (NO.17)
WAS KNOW AS "WHAT 'OPES?". THE HOUSE NEXT DOOR (NO.16) WAS "A LA POUPÉE". IT WAS
THE FAVOURITE RESTAURANT IN POP AND WAS "OFFICERS ONLY". THE SECRET OF
LA POUPÉE'S SUCCES WAS MADAME'S HOSPITALITY ,AND THE YOUTH
OF HER THREE DAUGHTERS. "GINGER", THE YOUNGEST DAUGHTER.
WAS WISE BEYOND HER 13 TO 15 YEARS AND WAS THE DARLING
OF MANY CUSTOMERS. IT'S STRIKING TO SEE HOW OFTEN
SHE FEATURES IN THE DIARIES OF OFFICERS WHO
STAYED IN POP FOR A WHILE.

PoP

Clayton, was not yet dead. He would die the day after Captain Staniland was killed. However shops and cafés flourished. Battalion histories and personal memoirs frequently mention the café *La Poupée* (The Doll) in the market square and the beautiful daughter 'Ginger' who served there; it was an 'Officers Only' establishment but there were plenty of other cafés. My Uncle Andrew in the 1/4th Lincolns certainly visited Poperinghe and probably also another uncle who came later in the war with a battalion of the 19th (Western) Division. My mother remembered one of her brothers describing the scene of women sitting at the front doors of their houses in Poperinghe, making lace and taking orders from soldiers for particular items which were to be collected on future visits. Mishaps at the front prevented some of the orders being collected.

However there were not many opportunities to visit places such as Poperinghe and, all in all, the men of the North Midland Division had moved from a genuinely quiet sector to one where their service would be more arduous and more dangerous.

Salient Action

All the dangers that had faced the men in the trenches below the Messines Ridge had to be faced again in the new sector, but with others added. The enemy in the trenches opposite were believed to be Saxons, probably no more warlike than the easy-going Bavarians encountered earlier, but they were driven harder by their commanders to wear down the new British arrivals by attrition.

The only benefit was that casualties due to rifle and machine-gun fire were lower. The British trenches were better constructed; the woods gave some shelter and the North Midland men had become more careful, but one lapse of care, and a German sniper could still snap up an unwary victim. Shelling became a much greater danger. The Germans seemed to have an unlimited supply of normal 5.9-inch high explosive shells – 'crumps' to the British soldiers – and used them freely. Barrages that searched to and fro along the British trenches and support positions took a steady toll. A Spalding man wrote home in September that 'about a thousand' shells fell in one day on the neighbouring Leicesters but only one man was killed and two wounded. But a 1/5th Lincolns' man said that one unexpected shell often caused more casualties than a barrage during which everyone had taken shelter. 'Minnies' or 'sausages' – explosive canisters thrown high into the air by a German mortar, a *Minnenwerfer* – were prevalent. The acute British shell shortage still continued, so there was little retaliation to the various types of German shelling.

A new German gun, not experienced at Messines, was to become a particular hazard here. This was a 'whizz-bang', a light field gun brought up by the Germans close to their trenches that fired a high velocity, flat trajectory shell which burst in the air just above its target. The heavier 'crumps' could be heard coming and the 'minnies' could be seen and often dodged, but the 'whizz-bang' arrived without warning, the 'whizz' of its approach and the 'bang' of its explosion being simultaneous. Most battalions ordered that no cooking fires were to be lit in their positions in daytime because the smoke often drew an instant 'whizz-bang'. The recently established North Midland Divisional Concert Party adopted the name 'The Whizz-Bangs' during this period.

The five men of the 1/4th Lincolns who were killed near Hill 60 on the battalion's second tour in the Salient trenches were all whizz-bang victims. The *Boston Guardian* quoted a letter from Private Woodham, one of its pre-war reporters, describing how Corporal Burchnall, the soldier from Freiston, had been killed. Burchnall had been in charge of a party of men who had been working all night carrying rations up to the front line and was now just behind the line preparing a mid-morning breakfast:

> *The scene at the time was a pleasant one; the men, in various states of undress, were boiling the water for tea, frying bacon and making ready for a hearty meal. The morning was sunny and bright, and everyone was in excellent spirits. Corporal Burchnall... was stooping down to pick up a piece of bacon, when a whizz-bang burst some thirty yards away. A piece of shrapnel struck him behind the ear and he fell back unconscious ... He only lived half an hour after being hit and never regained consciousness. There seems every reason to believe that his death was a painless one.* *

Private Woodham's account may well have been a faithful one on this occasion, but it should be borne in mind that letters from the front always tried to alleviate the feelings of relatives by glossing over the horrors of painful deaths.

The Germans had been here just long enough, since early May, to commence tunnelling operations for the placing of mines under the British trenches. No major explosions had been experienced yet but this type of

---

*A Town Remembers, William M. Hunt, p. 58.

A British front line trench wrecked by shell fire.

warfare would increase in coming months. The 1/4th Lincolns would not be seriously affected; the most serious incident would be suffered by one of the Sherwood Forester battalions almost at the end of their service on this sector, but this will be described later.

The trenches were sometimes so close together that grenades could be thrown from one to another. The Germans had enjoyed being supplied with better bombs than the British and in greater quantity, but the recently introduced and very effective British Mills grenade now saw the British with the better weapon. The battalion history of the 1/5th Lincolns records how their bombing officer, Lieutenant J S Nichols, angered by a German grenade attack, gathered a big stock of grenades and he and his men hurled a veritable fusillade into the German trench. This provoked a response a few hours later in the form of a message wrapped around a stone and thrown over from the German trench in these words:

> *Why on earth do you shoot so idiotically? If we are ordered to fling over two or three hand grenades, is it necessary for you to send immediately a dozen into our trenches? Stop this nonsense! My best friend has been killed because of this. Let us show ourselves in this great World War honourable, civilized human beings.* *

Is it a trait peculiar to the Germans to initiate some horror and then object when someone retaliates?

The Action at Hooge

There was only one outbreak of serious fighting in the vicinity of the North Midland Division during its three months of service on the Ypres Salient and it would only involve the Sherwood Forester Brigade.

Hooge, little more than a chateau, a chapel and a handful of houses on the Menin Road, lay just outside the Sherwood Forester Brigade's sector on the North Midland Division's left flank. It was a notorious 'hot spot', the possession of which was bitterly contested. (If one drives out along the Menin Road from Ypres and then past Hellfire Corner, it can be appreciated that if the Germans had possession of the rise ahead they would have observation over a large area of the British rear.) The British had always allocated a Regular division to hold that important place.

What became known as 'The Action at Hooge' commenced on 14 July with the explosion of a large British mine followed by an immediate attack by two battalions of the 3rd Division to occupy the crater and the nearby German trenches. Satisfied with this local success, Lieutenant General Allenby withdrew the 3rd Division from the line and replaced it with the New Army 14th (Light) Division which had earlier received its trench instruction from the North Midland Division. However the Germans were determined to regain their lost positions. In the early morning of 30 July they launched – for the first time in the war – a *Flammenwerfer,* or 'liquid fire', attack supported by a fierce infantry assault on the 14th Division's positions. The inexperienced Light Division battalions facing this horrific new weapon fell back.

The Sherwood Forester battalions on routine trench-holding duty in the line were the 1/8th Battalion (from the Nottinghamshire towns) and the 1/5th Battalion (Derby City). The German attack exposed the left flank of the brigade and also struck the trenches held by the 1/8th Battalion. It was a desperate situation but the Sherwood Foresters reacted in a most effective manner. The 1/8th Battalion fought off the attack on their trenches and also formed a flank defence. The 1/5th Battalion sent across its machine-guns

---

* *History of the 5th Battalion, The Lincolnshire Regiment,* Colonel T. E. Sandall, pp. 40-41

Hill 60 in 1915.

which did great execution by firing into the flank of the German attack on the 14th Division. The 1/7th Sherwood Foresters (Nottingham City) were called up from their brigade reserve position at Maple Copse with orders to fill the gap that had appeared on the division's left flank. Their Commanding Officer, Lieutenant Colonel C W Birkin, was seriously wounded by a shell burst before the battalion set off but a spare officer of the same rank, Lieutenant Colonel A W Brewill, was available and he led the battalion forward to this emergency task. The Nottingham men established a new line in the gap created by the German attack, helped fight off further German attacks, and then brought in many of the wounded 14th Division men from the battlefield.

The situation was eventually stabilized with the three Sherwood Forester battalions having performed extremely well in the first real fighting experienced by any part of the North Midland Division. The 1/8th Foresters, hit by the initial German attack, lost twenty-one men killed and forty wounded; the 1/7th Battalion had twelve men killed and about eighty wounded in their supporting operation. The award of several decorations followed. Lieutenant Colonel Brewill of the 1/7th Battalion received a DSO and among several other decorations in the same battalion was a DCM for Sergeant Charles Crawley who had featured prominently in the rescue of wounded from the battlefield. Crawley was a Boston born man who, in 1900, had been one of Meaburn Staniland's comrades in 'The Gallant Eight' from the local Volunteers who had gone off to the Boer War. 'The Action at

Hooge' was not a major battle, but was typical of the medium sized actions that could erupt anywhere on the Salient in the two years between the Second and Third Battles of Ypres.

As a result of its losses in the fighting, the Sherwood Forester Brigade was withdrawn from that sector later in August, its place being taken by the 3rd Division extending its right flank. The Lincolnshire-Leicestershire Brigade thus became the left-hand brigade in the North Midland Division but this had no effect on its experiences in the remaining few weeks of its time on the Salient. The Sherwood Foresters were moved to a quieter sector, taking over a brigade frontage from the 5th Division on the right of the North Midland Division. (See Map 2 on page 50.) Their new trenches were bounded by two well known features – The Dump just over the railway line from Hill 60, and The Bluff which was a mound created when the Ypres-Comines Canal had been constructed many years earlier to link the North Sea at Nieuport (now Nieuwpoort) with the great network of European trading canals. However this section of the canal was now choked by the debris of war and would never recover to come into service again.

The four Nottinghamshire and Derbyshire battalions would have six mainly uneventful weeks on that new sector to finish their time on the Salient. Casualties would be low – with the exception of one severe incident. On 30 September, in the brigade's last days there, the Germans blew a mine under a trench held by a platoon of the 1/6th Foresters, killing fifteen men and wounding most of the remainder of the platoon. The explosion was so violent that the bodies of eleven of the dead were never recovered. This battalion, from the outlying towns of Derbyshire, was the only one in the brigade to have missed the fighting at Hooge. Now its turn had come to lose valuable men, many of them the pre-war Territorials who had volunteered for overseas service and whose numbers were steadily diminishing throughout the division.

The Lost Cemeteries

On their earlier sector under the Messines Ridge the North Midland battalions had buried their dead in village churchyards or had made their own small battalion cemeteries in fields or at farms just behind the front. Conditions were different here. There was only one village immediately behind the divisional front, the battered Zillebeke. Its small churchyard contained a few graves from 1914 but there was little space remaining.

On their arrival, the battalions found that earlier British units had already

A small burial ground near the front line started by the 11th Hussars, cavalry serving as infantry, on the edge of a wood near Zillebeke in the early months of 1915. The North Midland Division units would have added their dead when they took over here in the summer.

A comrades' cemetery in winter mid-way through the war near some battered woodland in the Ypres Salient area, but the exact location is not known. IWM Q17849

established a chain of small burial plots, what I call 'comrades' cemeteries'. In much of the sector these could be located immediately behind the trench system because the large woods in British hands meant that the cemeteries on the western, or 'safe', side of the woods were concealed from German view. Where the ground was more open the cemeteries had to be a little further back. The North Midland battalions simply took over the cemeteries from the outgoing units, usually starting new rows or small plots to keep their graves separate from those of earlier units. When the Staffordshire Brigade settled down on the Hill 60 sector on the division's right flank, its battalions used two such cemeteries. The 1/5th South and 1/6th North Staffords, who routinely interchanged trench tours, used the cemetery at Blauwepoort Farm; the 1/6th South and 1/5th North Staffords used Larch Wood, where a small plot of graves was being made alongside the cutting of the railway line running back from Hill 60 to Ypres. Both of these cemeteries survived the war intact.

Unfortunately the exact locations and names of the cemeteries in the wooded areas further north cannot now be identified. It is believed that the Lincolnshire-Leicestershire Brigade, and the Sherwood Forester Brigade during its two months' service in the wooded sector, used up to five small cemeteries on the edge of or just inside Armagh Wood, Sanctuary Wood and Zouave Wood. One a little further back at Maple Copse was definitely used. However, in June 1916, one of the flare-ups that sporadically occurred on the Ypres Salient in the middle years of the war struck the area of the woods. The Canadians had been holding the front line here for several months. The Germans decided that they would force them off Tor Top (Hill 62) in Sanctuary Wood and also seize Mount Sorrel which was in No Man's Land near Armagh Wood. This they achieved in a fierce attack which captured the Canadian front line and an advance which reached as far as Maple Copse. The Canadians counterattacked two weeks later and regained most of the lost ground. The fierce fighting thus twice swept over the little cemeteries in which the Lincolns, Leicesters and Sherwood Foresters had buried their dead in 1915. Most of the cemeteries were destroyed and the one at Maple Copse was severely battered. The manner in which the Army Graves Service and the Imperial War Graves Commission treated the remains of the North Midland men they did find after the war will be described later, but it is a measure of the damage caused to those cemeteries that, of the North Midland men known to have been buried in the Armagh, Sanctuary and Zouave Woods areas in 1915, fewer than half now have graves in various post-war cemeteries. The remaining graves were completely lost and the men's names are on the Menin Gate Memorial to the Missing.

There was no such problem in the area between Hill 60 and the Canal to which the Sherwood Forester Brigade was moved at the end of August. Three small cemeteries were already established on or near the edge of some woodland behind the British trenches and the Forester battalions buried their trench casualties in two of these. The 1/5th and 1/6th – the two Derbyshire battalions – used Chester Farm and the 1/7th and 1/8th from Nottinghamshire used Hedge Row Trench Cemetery.

About 400 soldiers killed in and around the trenches were buried by their battalion comrades in those little cemeteries in or near the woods or at the farms during those three months in which the North Midland Division held that part of the Ypres Salient in the late summer of 1915. These were sad occasions, with the trenches only a couple of hundred yards or so away and the men never knowing who would be next to be wrapped in a blanket, covered with earth and have a rough wooden cross to mark his grave. It was earlier described how Corporal Burchnall, the Boston Company man killed by a 'whizz-bang' while having a late breakfast after a night's work of carrying supplies to the front line, had died. Now Private Woodham describes his friend's burial, a typical scene:

> *In the evening, amid a drizzle of rain, 'Charlie', as he was known to us all, was laid to rest in the little natural cemetery that has grown up by the railway line side, near the spot where he was killed, the last sad ceremony conducted amid the piping of bullets, and the everlasting whirring of the shells.** *

Corporal Burchnall and five other men of the 1/4th Lincolns were killed or fatally wounded near Hill 60 on the battalion's first tour in trenches in this sector in July. Four were buried in Larch Wood Cemetery and one in Railway Embankment Dugouts. Their graves survive in those cemeteries, but were to prove the only ones of the battalion to have been buried near the line and to survive the war undisturbed by the 1916 fighting. In September, the *Lincolnshire Standard* contained a report of the burial of one of its pre-war reporters, Lance Corporal Billy Smith, a Lincoln born man but well known in Boston and Horncastle where he had worked. He had been recommended for a commission but was killed early one morning after 'he had been harassing the Germans for the whole of the night at great personal risk'. He was buried the following night 'at a pretty spot in the shade of a wood in the moonlight'. But this was one of the cemeteries later lost and Billy Smith's name is one of those engraved on the Menin Gate Memorial.

Seven of the 1/4th Lincolns were killed in one incident on 2 September when companies of the battalion were in brigade reserve at the Railway Embankment Dugouts, normally a place of reasonable safety. According to the battalion war diary, 'German shelling was searching for artillery batteries in the neighbourhood' when a shell scored a direct hit on one of the dugouts. Three of the seven dead were from Boston and two each from Lincoln and Sleaford. Two of the Boston dead were sergeants, Ralph Parker and Albert Preston, and were undoubtedly close friends of my uncle. Sergeant Preston was a Boston born man but was in the Lincoln Company because he had worked in the city at Ruston and Proctor's engineering works before the war. He had been due to go home on leave to be married

---

A Town Remembers, William M. Hunt, p.58.

The communal grave of the seven men of the 1/4th Lincolns killed by shell fire at the Railway Embankment Dugouts. Transport Farm is in the background.

when he was killed. The seven men killed that day were buried side by side in a small cemetery that had been started near the railway embankment, the two Boston sergeants together.

Captain Staniland's Journey

The burial of one man was to take place in completely different and unusual circumstances.

It was very early in the morning of 29 July, a Thursday, the fourth day of what should have been a routine six-day tour but which would be extended to nine days because of the after-effects of the 'Action at Hooge' which would commence the following day. It had been a hectic and costly tour so far. The 46th Division was playing host to the battalions of a newly arrived New Army division, the 17th (Northern), for their trench instruction. A company of the 7th Green Howards had been attached to the 1/4th Lincolns for the first two days of the tour and then replaced by a company from the

7th Lincolns, Lincolnshire Territorials now playing hosts to Lincolnshire New Army men. There had been much German shelling and mortaring, and a small German mine had been exploded. The 1/4th Lincolns had lost seven men killed in the past three days, five from Lincoln and one each from Stamford and Grantham. Two of the Lincoln dead were brothers killed the same day: Privates Clarence and Percy Linnell, twenty-two and nineteen years of age respectively. (They are now buried side by side in Sanctuary Wood Cemetery, Plot 2, Row M.) Despite being in the front line, so far the Boston Company had been spared any serious losses.

Captain Staniland decided to go round the sentry posts in his company's line; he was probably following a regular routine to check that all was well in that pre-dawn period. All was quiet. He had been home on leave a month earlier. The *Lincolnshire Standard* had commented that he had 'looked the picture of good health, but was very reticent of saying anything concerning the doings of the troops at the front'. He was now one of the most experienced senior officers in the battalion. His commanding officer had been killed and all three of the other company commanders who had come out from England five months earlier had left the battalion, one wounded, one ill and one promoted into another battalion.

Meaburn Staniland reached a trench bay in which Lance Corporal John Short from Kirton and several other men from the Boston area had their posts. Lance Corporal Short's letter home, subsequently quoted in the *Lincolnshire Standard*, tells what happened next:

> I was in charge of a sentry group when the Captain came round. I should say about 3.45am, he stood on the firing platform in order to get a good look over the opposite trenches, as he would invariably have a good look round, and I was just getting up at his side when he staggered and fell, a bullet having struck him in the forehead. Myself and two others did all we could for him, but he passed away in the course of about three minutes.

Here again we have the description of the single bullet to the head and almost immediate death. Written to give solace to families when a death had actually been prolonged and painful. On this occasion other men's accounts of the results of that single shot are unanimously in agreement with the above account.

But the account was not complete. We have met, earlier, Meaburn Staniland's brother-in-law, Captain Arthur Hall, the officer in the 1st Dorsets who had played cricket with the 1/4th Lincolns at Locre. His battalion was still in Belgium and Hall, a Lincolnshire man, had almost certainly been able to keep in touch with Meaburn Staniland and his fellow Lincolns officers. On the day that Staniland was killed, the 1st Dorsets were out of the line, resting at farms around the village of Watou, three miles west of Poperinghe. The Dorsets were due to leave this area as part of the 5th Division which was to be transferred to the Somme to take over a sector of

This is the only known photograph of Captain Staniland taken during his period of service in Belgium. He is using a rangefinder from a reserve trench during the period when the 1/4th Lincolns were on the Messines Ridge sector. He is accompanied by CSM Peasgood.

line there previously held by the French. The 1/4th Lincolns' transport lines were at Poperinghe and it is reasonable to assume that news of his brother-in-law's death would have swiftly reached Arthur Hall at Watou. It is known that he did not proceed with his battalion to the Somme when it departed from Watou on the following day.

Arthur Hall probably played a key role in the events immediately following Meaburn Staniland's death and would have discussed the manner of the death with the Lincolns' officers. He later told his son what really happened: 'It was during the night. He was standing on the step and his last words were, "By God, I'm going to have a pipe." He struck a match, and then came the shot.'*

It may not have been the first time that Meaburn Staniland had been tempted to light his pipe when visiting that particular sentry post. It is unlikely to have been a stray shot. A German sniper was probably waiting patiently for the flare-up of a match and had got off a perfect shot. Letters home from Staniland's men were censored by the company officers, and men going on leave would have been told not to discuss the details of their company commander's death at home. There must have been some loose talk, however, because a strange rumour later circulated in Boston to the effect that Meaburn Staniland had taken his own life, a suggestion that was so outlandish that it gained no credence.

All published reports of Meaburn Staniland's death refer to it as having been 'at Hooge' but this was an inaccurate generalization. It could loosely be termed the Hooge sector, but the war diary states that the battalion was occupying Trenches 50 to A7. This was a length of the front line about 600 yards long, partly on the forward edge of Armagh Wood and partly on open ground on a downward slope in front of the wood. (See Map 2 on page 50.) A track named earlier by a British rifle regiment battalion as Green Jacket Drive ran right through a shallow valley in No Man's Land in front of the Lincolns' trench. The German front line was just across the valley on or near the edge of a wood called Shrewsbury Forest. But we can be more precise. Lance Corporal Kent kept a small diary which has survived and the entry for 27 July, 'A1 to 50', shows that the Boston Company was holding the extreme right of the battalion frontage. Mount Sorrel was close by on the right. Hooge was a mile and a quarter away to the north. The village of Zillebeke was closer, a mile away behind the line.

Meaburn Staniland's body was probably carried back by stretcher to the Regimental Aid Post where his fatal wound was cleaned, his personal belongings removed for return to his wife and the body then left covered by a blanket all day while the complex arrangements were being made for his burial. It was a quiet period and the 1/4th Lincolns suffered no further fatal casualties in their trenches that day. The Germans were preparing the

*From an interview with Rear Admiral Geoffrey Hall, Arthur Hall's son, 13 August 2002.

'liquid-fire' attack that would commence at Hooge in a few hours' time. It would be in this attack that Lieutenant Gilbert Talbot would be killed, to give his name immortality at Talbot House in Poperinghe. Platoons of Talbot's battalion, the 7th Rifle Brigade in the 14th (Light) Division had earlier been attached to the 1/4th Lincolns for trench instruction and it is possible that Talbot and Staniland had met at that time.

The 1/4th Lincolns did, however, suffer one more death the day that Captain Staniland was killed. It was another officer, but he was not in the trenches at the time of his death. Second Lieutenant Wilfred Fox was a young man from Horncastle, son of a deceased corn merchant and his widowed mother. He had been at Oxford University on the outbreak of war, but had immediately come home and joined the local Territorials as a private. Having passed through an Officer Training Corps while at public school, he was soon commissioned and had 'gone out' as a reinforcement officer to the 1/4th Lincolns in May. He had just been home on his first leave and was coming up to rejoin his company in the trenches when he was hit by a random German shell and, according to what

Talbot House, Poperinghe. Named after Lieutenant Gilbert Talbot

might have been the usual euphemistic letter home, had 'died instantaneously'. So the battalion lost two of its officers on one day.

I cannot pretend that what follows is an exact description of the events leading up to Meaburn Staniland's burial. Only a few key facts are known, but the following reconstruction is a feasible one. If what actually happened differs from it, then the differences will be neither large nor important.

There was almost certainly a 'comrades' cemetery' close to the Armagh Wood trenches, though it was one of those that would have been badly damaged in the fighting a year later. The graves of the seven other ranks of the 1/4th Lincolns killed so far in this trench tour, and of five more who would die later in the tour, were all recovered after the war and are now buried in a concentration plot in Sanctuary Wood Cemetery, somewhat to the north of their original burial location. There was, however, no precedent for the burial of officers of the North Midland Division killed during their service on the Ypres Salient sector. As it was the practice of taking the bodies of officers back from the line for separate burial had virtually ceased; it was certainly not convenient to do so in the crowded areas behind the Salient. The only infantry officer to die in the division so far on this sector was Lieutenant Frank Tarr, adjutant of the 1/4th Leicesters, a very popular pre-war rugby international, who had been killed two weeks earlier by a shell fragment which struck him in the face while visiting the brigade reserve position at the Zillebeke Lake Dugouts. He had later been buried in the small cemetery which had been started at the Railway Embankment Dugouts. Where should Captain Staniland and Second Lieutenant Fox be buried? In the nearby cemetery where the other ranks were being buried? In the brigade reserve position at the Railway Embankment Dugouts with Lieutenant Tarr? Or at the distant, dull little village of Ouderdom where the battalion went when allowed a proper rest period, but which had no church or churchyard? (Grootebeek British Cemetery, just outside Ouderdom, was not started until 1917).

The grave of Lieutenant Frank Tarr who was killed when struck in the face by a small fragment of shell at the Zillebeke Lake Dugouts; it would have caused only a minor wound if it had struck any other part of his body. He was a Leicester solicitor and also a celebrated rugby player, appearing 94 times for Leicester Tigers and four times for England at centre threequarter.

The decision was taken that Captain Staniland's body would be transported to Dranoutre where both his brother and his former commanding officer had been buried in the churchyard during the battalion's earlier spell of duty in the trenches under the Messines Ridge. Perhaps Meaburn Staniland had expressed a wish that, if he were killed, he would like to be buried there. His brother-in-law Arthur Hall probably took a prominent part in the planning. His son states, 'My father would have moved heaven and earth to see that Meaburn was reunited with his brother'. This suggestion would have received sympathetic support from Major Oliver Cooper, Staniland's old Boer War comrade from Boston and from the current Lincolns commanding officer, Lieutenant Colonel Barrell. He had once been the commander of the Spalding Territorial Company and had been a close colleague of Meaburn Staniland over many years. Attention then turned to the arrangements for the burial of Second Lieutenant Fox. It was decided that the young officer's body should also travel to Dranoutre so that the graves of all of the battalion's officers killed so far could be kept together in the churchyard of that friendly village.

The journey to Dranoutre and the burial arrangements would be complicated. It was a hectic and stressful time. The heavy fighting at Hooge would disrupt communications in the rear and would cause the Lincolns' present tour in the trenches to be extended to last a further five days. Lieutenant Colonel Barrell was a sick man with stomach trouble due to drinking polluted water and would be evacuated to England four days after Captain Staniland's death. This left Major Cooper in temporary command of the battalion. A diary kept by one of the soldiers, Lance Corporal Noel Gardiner, also states that the Adjutant, Captain Johnson, was 'suffering from nerves' at that time, so the battalion's leadership must have been fully stretched that day. A burial party would have to be provided and transport arranged to a village nine miles away. The journey there would have to cut across the lines of communication of three other divisions. To say 'nine miles', with today's modern vehicles and good roads, does not sound like a long journey, but it certainly was under the conditions of the time. It is surprising that orders did not come down from above that the 1/4th Lincolns should abandon the plans being made and bury the two officers in the nearest cemetery.

However the plans were approved and the arrangements completed. The bodies were wrapped in blankets which were then bound with rope. A message had probably been sent back to the 'rear details' in the transport lines that were ten miles back at Poperinghe to send a working party to Dranoutre to dig the graves. The bodies were carried by stretcher to a point behind the trenches to which the battalion's transport wagons delivered rations and stores, then loaded onto one of them for the first part of the road journey. Whether the same wagon then went the whole way to Dranoutre is not known. Perhaps the Boston Territorial Artillery Battery, which was much better provided with transport, took over at some convenient spot like Zillebeke or Shrapnel Corner. The battery's pre-war commander, Captain Oswald Giles, was another Boston solicitor. Perhaps the divisional Army Service Corps provided a lorry. Whoever it was, the next stage of the journey was down the long, straight Ypres-Kemmel road. The journey was probably made at night because much of that road was under German observation. It is known that a rendezvous was arranged at Lindenhoek where the transport would have to leave the main road and travel through narrow lanes to Dranoutre. In their earlier spell of duty in this area, the 1/4th Lincolns had never made the journey from Lindenhoek direct to Dranoutre. The Battalion HQ at Lindenhoek Chalet had only been on the route to the trenches when the battalion had been using Locre as its billeting village. This is probably why Lance Corporal Kent was sent to Lindenhoek to guide the transport carrying the bodies on that final stage through the country lanes across the lower slopes of Mount Kemmel to Dranoutre.

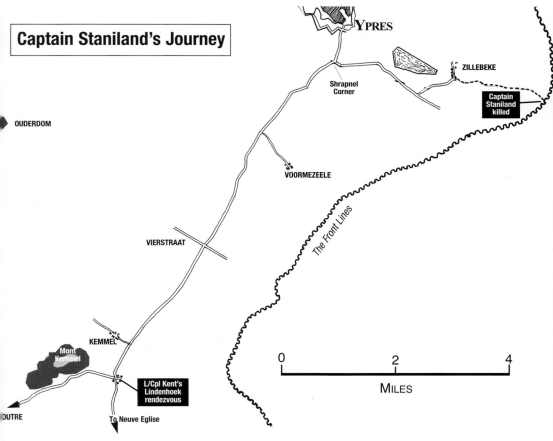

Captain Staniland's Journey

YPRES

ZILLEBEKE

Shrapnel
Corner

Captain
Staniland
killed

OUDERDOM

VOORMEZEELE

The Front Lines

VIERSTRAAT

KEMMEL

Mont
Kemmel

L/Cpl Kent's
Lindenhoek
rendezvous

OUTRE

To Neuve Eglise

0   2   4

MILES

Why was Lance Corporal Kent involved? Before the war he had worked with his father at their monumental mason's business near Boston Cemetery. Undoubtedly the Kents had many dealings with Meaburn Staniland, the local solicitor who handled the estates of deceased clients and who was the town clerk whose department allocated burial plots in the cemetery. William Kent had been a pre-war Territorial in Captain Staniland's company. The two families were probably also friends, although Meaburn Staniland, at thirty-three, was ten years older than William Kent. His pre-war association with his dead company commander and his familiarity with funeral procedures made him an obvious choice to be detached from trench duty to take part. He may have inscribed the two wooden crosses being prepared to mark the graves. His tiny diary, which never goes into detail, merely has 'Captain Staniland' for the day of his company commander's death. There is no indication in any diary or document, or in any letter home quoted in the local press, as to when the burials actually took place.

One surprise had greeted the burial party at Dranoutre. When the 1/4th Lincolns left that area in June to move up to the Ypres Salient, the narrow strip of ground at the side of Dranoutre churchyard had only contained the graves of five officers, four from their own battalion and one from the divisional Royal Engineers. But, since then, other units had added nine further British graves. The first three of these had been of officers, in what had been intended to be an officers-only plot, but then battalions of the 28th Division had buried six private soldiers because all other spaces in the churchyard had become full. So, whereas Second Lieutenant Geoffrey Staniland's had been the first grave in that head-to-toe line, his brother Meaburn had to be buried in the fifteenth grave space, a hundred yards further back. Second Lieutenant Fox was buried behind Captain Staniland and a lance corporal of the 2nd Buffs (The East Kents), who died the day after the two Lincolns' officers, was buried behind Second Lieutenant Fox. It is not known who conducted the burial service for the two Lincolns' officers. Perhaps the Buffs' lance corporal shared a funeral service with them. They were the last British soldiers to be buried in Dranoutre churchyard.

Bad News Reaches Boston

Meaburn Staniland had been killed on a Thursday. It was late on the following Saturday evening when an official telegram containing brief details of his death reached his home at Wyberton, just outside Boston. The following day a letter from Lieutenant Colonel Barrell provided more details.

The next issue of the *Lincolnshire Standard*, on the following Saturday, describes the effect in Boston of the death of this prominent citizen: the council held a special meeting; there was a public meeting where ordinary people could express their tributes; various entertainments were cancelled as a mark of respect; special services were held in several churches. At the one in Wyberton Parish Church on Thursday, Captain Arthur Hall was able to attend, obviously having been granted compassionate leave to support his sister, Meaburn's widow, and her four small sons, the youngest of whom, another Meaburn, was only thirteen months old. No other event in the war was given as much coverage in the Boston edition of the *Lincolnshire Standard* as the death of Captain Staniland – more than five columns, a total of 112 column inches. 'Sentinel', the leader writer, used the language of the day to sum up the mood of the town:

> *One event of this week has overshadowed all else. The news late on Saturday evening that Captain Meaburn Staniland, the gallant soldier Town Clerk of Boston, had fallen victim to a German sniper, came as a terrible shock. On Sunday people spoke of the awful tragedy in subdued*

tones and with bated breath. Aye, and more often than not, with a tear-bedimmed eye. It was as though a heavy pall, thick and impenetrable, had fallen over the town. I had the opportunity of seeing the effect of the news upon various grades of our public and social scale. It was all the same. Intense sorrow everywhere. Boston was a grief-stricken town, genuine, ineffable, unspeakable.

After the special council meeting, the council had to meet again to appoint a replacement town clerk and Meaburn's father, Lieutenant Colonel R. W. Staniland, his predecessor in this post, was recalled to the position. Another piece in the same *Standard* that reported all these events was a letter from the front to show that Meaburn Staniland's position there as company commander had also been filled quickly.

2nd August 1915.

Dear Mr Goodacre, I deeply regret having to report that your son, Pte. A. Goodacre, was killed on the 31 July, about 3 a.m., while doing his duty like a good soldier in the trenches.

He was shot through the heart by a shrapnel bullet, and must have died instantly. Mr Beaulah, his Platoon Officer, tells me he was always a very cool, conscientious, soldier. Both officers and men will miss him very much. He was buried in the Military Cemetery just behind the lines.

Deeply sympathising with you in your great loss.

I am,
Yours sincerely,
CHAS. GRAY, Capt.,
Officer Commanding "A" Co., 4th Batt., Lincolnshire Regt.

It was not one of the Boston officers who had been selected to replace Meaburn Staniland as commander of the still mainly Boston Company, but an officer from the Stamford Company. (Private Arthur Goodacre, is now buried in Sanctuary Wood Cemetery, Plot 4, Row P.)

The Final Weeks in the Salient

The 1/4th Lincolns remained in the trenches for five more days after Captain Staniland was killed. The roar of the fighting at Hooge could be heard on the left. Increased German shelling on the trenches near Armagh Wood killed another five men in the battalion, giving a fatal casualty list for that tour of two officers and twelve men killed and at least four more dying of their wounds later. It was the worst trench tour in the battalion's entire first six months of active service. 'B' Company of the 7th Lincolns, attached for five days of instruction, lost seven men killed or died of wounds during the same period.

The widowed Mrs Frances Staniland in the garden of her parents' home at Manby, near Louth, in November 1915 with three of her sons – twins Jack and Bob (left and right) and Jim, and her brother, Major Arthur Hall of the Dorsets, on leave from France. It is too cold for the youngest boy, seventeen-months-old Meaburn, to be outside.

The 1/4th Lincolns served five more trench tours before the North Midland Division left the Salient for a new duty, but the main events have all been covered. When they marched out of the trenches in the early hours of 2 October, handing over to the 2nd Royal Irish Rifles, 3rd Division, they had spent ninety-seven days and nights in this area, forty-nine of them in eight trench tours, twenty in brigade reserve and only twenty-eight days at Ouderdom, many of those days seeing large working parties being sent to dig reserve trenches.

One other battalion officer died after Captain Staniland and Second Lieutenant Fox. This was Second Lieutenant Leslie Reed, born in Louth but working in a bank at Horncastle before the war and a pre-war member of the Territorials there. He was killed as he emerged from a dug-out on 27 August by a projectile described as 'an aerial torpedo', probably another name for a *Minnenwerfer*. He was buried among ordinary soldiers in the little cemetery at the Railway Embankment Dugouts (Plot 1, Row C). Of five officers from Horncastle to have come out to Belgium six months earlier, four were now dead; only Captain Arthur Ellwood, whose brother Charles had been killed in June, remained. The battalion's total fatalities on the Salient were three officers – more than any other battalion in the division – and fifty-four other ranks. Of the dead with identifiable homes, twenty-six came from the Lincoln area, eleven from Boston, five from Grantham, three each from Horncastle and Stamford, and two each from Spalding and Sleaford. That figure of fifty-seven dead in three months on the Ypres Salient was more than double the fatal loss in the earlier period of the same length in the trenches under the Messines Ridge.

In addition to its dead, the battalion had seen a considerable number of its men evacuated as wounded, sick or suffering from various forms of stress. Exact figures for casualties from these causes for the 1/4th Lincolns were not recorded, but comparisons

Killed by a sniper on his first morning in the front line.

3476 PRIVATE
B. UPCRAFT
LINCOLNSHIRE REGIMENT
15TH SEPTEMBER 1915

EGYPT
LINCOLNSHIRE

with published figures in the post-war histories of other battalions in the North Midland Division indicate a loss of at least 200 men of all ranks. (The 1/4th Lincolns was one of the only battalions in the division which did not publish a post-war history.) Like every other unit in the division, the battalion was now very weak in strength. Territorial recruiting at home had fallen away with the rise in popularity of Kitchener's New Army, particularly when the 'Pals' Battalions movement gained momentum in late 1914 and early 1915. The only reference in the 1/4th Lincolns war diary to a reinforcement draft being received during this period was on 6 September when eighty-two men arrived. The 1/4th Leicesters, receiving a draft at about the same time, refused to accept a quarter of the new men because they were considered insufficiently trained! One of that 6 September draft for the 1/4th Lincolns, Private Burton Upcraft, a Boston man but working for the Great Northern Railway at Lincoln when he volunteered for the Territorials in December 1914, was killed by a sniper on his first morning in the trenches. (He is now buried in Ypres Reservoir Cemetery, Plot 7, Row A). Those few reinforcements, to replace 250 casualties of various kinds, meant that every three remaining soldiers in the battalion now had to hold the section of trench previously held by, or carry out the work of, four men who had come to the Salient in June or of five men who had come out to Belgium in March.

The shortage was particularly severe among the battalion officers. A report in the *Lincolnshire Standard* in mid-August showed that, of the thirty-three officers who had gone out with the battalion in March, only nine remained at that time. It has been described how Lieutenant Colonel Barrell had been invalided home in July. His second-in-command, Major Oliver Cooper, took over command for the next five weeks but was not confirmed in that position and had to give way in September to a Regular officer, Lieutenant Colonel C. E. Heathcote of the King's Own Yorkshire Light Infantry, who was posted in to become the battalion's fourth commanding officer in four months. Lance Corporal Noel Gardiner, a Boston man, referred to the new CO in his diary as 'a bit of a martinet, a good soldier but one who treated his men like dogs'. It was the classic case of a Regular sent in to 'smarten up' a Territorial battalion. Colonel Gilbert Barrell, however, later came out again from England and resumed command of the battalion in June 1916 until the end of that year when further illness forced his permanent return home. At company level, Captain Staniland had been the last of the original company commanders. Of the other pre-war Boston officers, Lieutenants Harold Marris and Ted Beaulah were both back in England, Marris with 'nervous exhaustion' and Beaulah for 'surgical treatment'. Major Cooper was the only pre-war Boston officer still with the battalion. One of the other ranks to be invalided home was Lance Corporal

William Kent. He became ill with enteric fever within three weeks of helping to bury Captain Staniland and was sent to a base hospital at Etaples. Despite seven weeks of treatment and was eventually evacuated to England.

The great British offensive by six divisions at Loos opened on 25 September. The North Midland battalions which were in the line in the Sanctuary Wood-Armagh Wood area at that time played a small part in the diversionary activity carried out on the Ypres Salient to deceive the Germans and stop them moving reserves down to Loos. The 3rd and 14th (Light) Divisions carried out mock attacks around Hooge, while the North Midland battalions placed damp straw in front of their trenches to be lit to resemble the discharge of gas. However it was raining and most of the straw became too wet to burn. The two Lincolnshire battalions were not in the line at the time and took no part in these moves, and were thus spared the angry German artillery reply.

It was almost the end for the North Midland Division in the Ypres Salient. Most of its line was handed over to the 17th (Northern) Division. As they came out of the line, the battalions realized that a move was afoot. They did not go back to Ouderdom, but to other places of rest. All leave was stopped. The battalions were visited by the corps commander, Lieutenant General Allenby, who thanked them for their services while under his command. Lieutenant Colonel R E Martin of the 1/4th Leicesters took the opportunity to complain to the general about the poor quality of training of the new officers being sent to his battalion. One by one, the battalions marched to Abeele Station, the last stop on the line from the coast to Poperinghe, and entrained for a new area. They travelled south into France.

What had the North Midland Territorials accomplished during their six months of service in Belgium? The division had held two substantial sectors of the front line satisfactorily, though the Germans had made no effort to dislodge them. The only actual fighting had been experienced by three battalions of the Sherwood Foresters who had acquitted themselves well during the 'Action at Hooge'. All battalions had carried out a massive amount of digging and the division reckoned that it now had an exemplary reputation as a constructor of sound defence works in trenches, work which would benefit later tenants of those trenches. The men had been sniped, shelled, *minniwerfered*, showered with hand grenades and blown up by underground mines, all at the hands of a professional enemy well supplied with stocks of ammunition. They had been rained upon, drenched in storms and laboured under a sweltering sun, but they had not had to endure the frost and snow of winter trench holding. That miserable experience awaited the men who would survive what was to come in the next week.

They had inflicted an unknown number of casualties on the Germans in the trenches opposite, but had certainly suffered more losses themselves from hostile action and through sickness aggravated by the difficulty of these Territorial soldiers in coping with the strain of prolonged active service and poor hygienic conditions. They had, however, become experienced in all aspects of defensive trench holding and had passed on that experience to two newer divisions. But, they had learned nothing of offensive action. This lack of experience was shortly to be rectified.

What had been the cost? The exact number of dead – killed in action and died of wounds or sickness – in the infantry battalions is known. During the recent Ypres Salient tour, the North Midland Division had lost twelve officers and 505 other ranks in fatal casualties in its battalions. The Sherwood Forester Brigade and the Lincolnshire-Leicestershire Brigade had suffered almost equal fatal casualties – 189 and 188 men respectively. The Sherwood Foresters had suffered heavily in the fighting at Hooge; the 1/4th Lincolns and their trench-alternating partners of the 1/5th Leicesters seem to have attracted more than their fair share of shelling and mine explosions to incur nearly two-thirds of their brigade's casualties. The Hill 60 sector had not proved to be as dangerous as its reputation warranted the Staffordshire Brigade, which had been in the trenches there for most of the period, had only lost 140 dead, the second time this brigade had suffered the fewest casualties.

Now that the North Midland Division had relinquished its trench-holding duty and was leaving Belgium, its fatal infantry casualties in its entire first six months of active service can be listed.

	Officers	Other Ranks	Total
137 Brigade			
1/5th North Staffords (Stoke and Potteries)	5	66	71
1/6th North Staffords (Burton-on-Trent)	2	64	66
1/5th South Staffords (Walsall area)	1	50	51
1/6th South Staffords (Wolverhampton)	3	60	63
Total	11	240	251
138 Brigade			
1/4th Lincolns (south of the county)	7	79	86
1/5th Lincolns (north of the county)	2	75	77
1/4th Leicesters (Leicester city)	6	68	74
1/5th Leicesters (county towns)	4	85	89
Total	19	307	326

139 Brigade

1/5th Sherwood Foresters (Derby city)	None	64	64
1/6th Sherwood Foresters (county towns)	3	90	93
1/7th Sherwood Foresters (Nottingham city)	2	58	60
1/8th Sherwood Foresters (county towns)	4	119	123
Total	9	331	340
46th (North Midland) Division – *Total*	39	878	917

The Sherwood Forester Brigade had suffered the most fatal casualties and its 1/8th Battalion again, as in the first three months, sustained the greatest battalion loss. The 1/4th Lincolns had lost the most officers and was still the only battalion to have had a battalion commander killed. By contrast, the 1/5th Sherwood Foresters had suffered no fatal officer casualty at all yet and would not do so until March 1916. It was an almost unknown occurrence for an infantry battalion to spend a year without a single officer being killed. If a rough figure of about 2,750 further casualties for non-fatal wounds and sickness are added to the dead during the past six months, the division had suffered a total casualties list of nearly 3,700 infantrymen, or approximately one-third of the mostly pre-war Territorials who had sailed from England in February. Such a casualty list was not excessive by First World War standards for a division holding trenches in spring and summer conditions. Routine 'wastage' was the military term, although the figures for the North Midland battalions may have been higher than usual as the result of their initial inexperience and later the above average dangers encountered on the Ypres Salient.

The last man to die in the 1/4th Lincolns was my uncle, Sergeant Andrew Crick, platoon sergeant of No. 1 Platoon, 'A' Company – the mainly Boston company. He was badly wounded on 30 September, the last full day that his battalion spent in the trenches. The battalion war diary says that at 6.30pm the Germans carried out some 'severe whizz-banging' on trenches 49, 50, A1 and A2. This was the same trench line at Armagh Wood where Captain Staniland had been sniped two months earlier. One man had been killed and nine wounded. The dead man was Private George Mann, from Lincoln; his grave was later lost. One of the wounded, Lance Corporal Lewis Hughes from Stamford, was evacuated to a base hospital at Etaples where he died three days later and was buried in the large cemetery there (Plot 3, Row B). My uncle was sent back no further than No. 10 Casualty Clearing Station at Remy Farm, near Poperinghe.

Abbé Tiberghien, a French padre at Remy Farm, Second Lieutenant Basil

Wood, my uncle's platoon commander, and Sister Roscoe of the Casualty Clearing Station all wrote letters to my grandparents' home in Hartley Street warning that the wound, 'in the lower abdomen' according to Sister Roscoe, was very serious. After languishing for five days, he died at 7.30am on 6 October, by which time his comrades in the 1/4th Lincolns were twenty-five miles away in France near Béthune, on the approaches to the Loos battlefield. Sister Roscoe and Abbé Tiberghien wrote again, the nursing sister describing how he died, the priest saying that he had buried my uncle in a cemetery that the French had started near the farm. His grave is in Plot 1, Row B of what is now Lijssenthoek Military Cemetery. An appendix will provide more information on that interesting cemetery.

My mother was deeply affected by the First World War. She was the youngest of six children. Sergeant Crick was the oldest. A second brother was taken prisoner and slightly gassed in the German March offensive in 1918 while serving in the 8th Gloucesters, 19th (Western) Division. He later died of chronic bronchitis. Her eldest sister was at Mons on the outbreak of war, working as governess to a little girl at a chateau at the nearby village of Hyon where some of the fighting of the battle on 23 August 1914 took place. She was then cut off in Belgium, under German control, until

Died of wounds – Sergeant Crick's grave. The headstones in Lijssenthoek are not of the normal white Portland Stone but of the darker Hopton Wood stone.

repatriated by the Red Cross a few days before the end of the war. Her father died in a failed medical operation in 1918. My grandfather's death led to the winding up of the prosperous building firm my grandfather had carried on before the war with my Uncle Andrew. It was my mother's stories of Sergeant Crick's pre-war rifle shooting successes, his time in the trenches in 1915 and then his death, that aroused my interest in the war and it was a visit to the Western Front in 1967 to see his grave and some of the battlefields that launched me onto an unexpected new career that has lasted more than thirty years.

PART FOUR

The Years That Followed

The main part of my story is over; it is not my intention to write the complete war history of the Boston Territorial Company, of the 1/4th Lincolns, or of the 46th (North Midland) Division. Having covered the first six months of their service on the Western Front, all I wish to do now is to describe briefly the subsequent experiences of the North Midland units and of some of the men and families already mentioned.

The Hohenzollern Redoubt

The Battle of Loos opened before the North Midland Division left the Ypres Salient and spluttered on with little British gain for two weeks. The division arrived in the area and received orders to carry out an attack on a network of German trenches known as the Hohenzollern Redoubt near the foot of one of the slagheaps in this coalmining area. Most of the redoubt had been captured on the first day of the battle but had then been recaptured by the Germans. It dominated newly won British trenches nearby and its successful capture now would enable the battle to be closed down.

The North Midland Division was to attack on a two-brigade frontage in broad daylight on the afternoon of 13 October and capture the redoubt, the slagheap and a nearby miners' housing estate, and then form a new line beyond all these objectives, a total advance of one mile. The divisional commander objected to the plan, saying that he would prefer to capture the redoubt by 'siege methods', but this was refused and he was ordered to carry out the frontal attack. Presumably because the Sherwood Foresters had sustained more casualties on the Ypres Salient than the other brigades, their battalions were given a supporting role in the plan, holding firm the jumping off trenches and then following up later to consolidate the anticipated gains. This left the Lincolnshire-Leicestershire and Staffordshire Brigades to carry out the main attack. Also involved in the attack were the 1/1st Monmouths, a Territorial unit that had recently joined the division as the Pioneer Battalion with which all infantry divisions were now augmented. No other division would be taking any substantial part in the attack.

The basic story can quickly be told. A short artillery preparation proved ineffective. Advancing in successive waves, the attacking battalions were cut down by machine-gun and rifle fire as soon as they left their trenches. Only a handful of the Lincolns and Leicesters reached and entered the redoubt where confused fighting continued for the next two days, with some of the

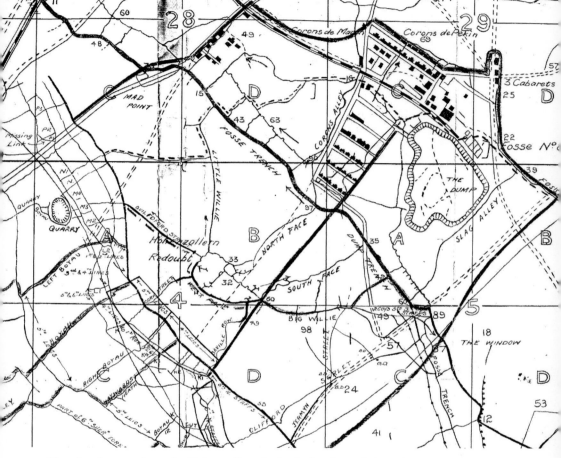

Plan for the attack on the Hohenzollern Redoubt by the 46th Division.

Sherwood Foresters later becoming involved there. The gains proved to be untenable and the survivors holding out in the redoubt were eventually withdrawn to the original front line. It was the sort of wildly optimistic and badly planned attack that gave First World War generalship a bad name.

The division rendered a total casualty return of 180 officers and 3,583 other ranks killed, missing and wounded; most of the 'missing' were dead. The average casualty rate in the six battalions carrying out the main attack was approximately 65 per cent. The detailed breakdown of the 1/4th Lincolns' casualties is typical of those battalions. Out of fourteen officers and 600 other ranks that went into action, six officers and 166 other ranks

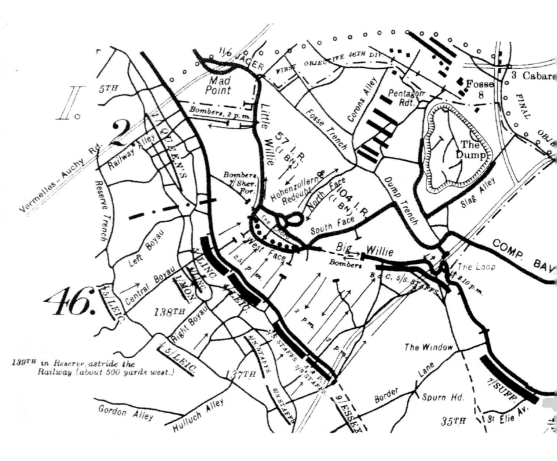

Official History map showing the disastrous attack.

(28 per cent) were killed and four officers and 219 other ranks (36 per cent) were wounded. Two battalion commanders were killed – Lieutenant Colonel John Knight of the 1/5th North Staffords in circumstances that were never established – he was not seen again after going 'over the top', and Lieutenant Colonel George Fowler of the 1/8th Sherwood Foresters, killed in the final hours of the fighting in the Hohenzollern Redoubt. Every one of the officers of the 1/4th Leicesters became a casualty. When the remnants of that battalion returned to their billets under an NCO on the evening of the 15th, just two officers, the Quartermaster and the Transport Officer, neither of whom had taken part in the battle, sat down to a silent dinner in the Officers' Mess; 'they dare not look at each other' wrote the battalion historian later.

Among the killed in the 1/4th Lincolns were Captain Charles Gray who had taken over the Boston Company when Captain Staniland was killed, Captain William Johnson, commander of the Stamford Company who had been wounded earlier but had returned to duty, and Second Lieutenant Basil Wood who, only twelve days earlier, had been writing to Boston about my uncle's death. Nine Territorials from the Boston Company and four from the Boston Artillery Battery were killed. One of the Lincoln casualties was Private Basil Crick, first cousin of my Uncle Andrew. Major Oliver Cooper, the last remaining pre-war Boston officer, had both arms smashed by shrapnel. Sergeant Charles Crawley, another of the 'Gallant Eight' who went to the Boer War with Oliver Cooper and Meaburn Staniland and who had recently won a DCM at Hooge with the 1/7th Sherwood Foresters, was killed. A tragic loss in the 1/5th Lincolns was the deaths of forty-nine-year-old Lance Corporal William John Livingstone Anderson of Grimsby and his nineteen-year-old son, Private Anderson, who had the same three Christian names as his father. A second son was killed with the 10th Lincolns – the Grimsby Chums – at Arras in 1917. (Of the fatal casualties named above, only Captain Johnson has an identified grave. He died of wounds two days after the attack and is buried in Béthune Town Cemetery, Plot 2, Row K).

Despite the failure of the attack, some decorations were awarded. Two Victoria Crosses were won. The first was not by a 46th Division man but by Corporal James Dawson of the Royal Engineers who saved some infantrymen from being gassed by removing some leaking gas cylinders while under fire. The second VC was awarded to twenty-one-year-old Captain Charles Vickers of the 1/7th Sherwood Foresters, the Nottingham City Battalion, for gallantry in the fighting in the Hohenzollern Redoubt on the second day of the division's battle. He was severely wounded but recovered, returned to service, and eventually reached the rank of colonel. From the 1/4th Lincolns, Captain Arthur Ellwood, the last surviving pre-

Captain Charles Vickers

war Horncastle officer, now in command of the brigade machine-guns, won a DSO for organizing the defence of a captured part of the Hohenzollern Redoubt, and Company Sergeant Major Peasgood, who had taken the Boston Company to war earlier in the year, won a DCM.

It had been a double disaster for the North Midland Division. Its first attempt to attack had been a failure and the cost had been unduly severe. The casualties at the Hohenzollern Redoubt, mostly incurred in those first few minutes of the attack, exceeded the division's entire casualty list for the six months of its earlier service holding the trenches under the Messines Ridge and on the Ypres Salient. The number of dead was particularly high – almost one and a half times the total for its earlier first six months. The

The Boston edition of the Lincolnshire Standard *reports the Hohenzollern Redoubt casualties.*

pre-war Territorial content of the infantry battalions had been dealt a massive blow and would now be a steadily diminishing minority.

The small area of ground in front of the trenches from which the battalions had attacked the Hohenzollern Redoubt was not fought over again and remained No Man's Land almost to the end of the war. Only the bodies of the men who had been killed by shellfire while in the British-held trenches or who later died of wounds were given proper burial. Those killed on the battlefield remained in the open, exposed to the elements and to casual shellfire for three years, and few of them could be recognized when the ground was cleared after the war. I took a sample hundred names of the dead from the attacking battalions and found that only five had identified graves. This means that over a thousand men have no known graves and are listed under their regiments on the Loos Memorial to the Missing on the walls of Dud Corner Cemetery. There is no local military cemetery or memorial to the fighting at the Hohenzollern Redoubt, the small Quarry Cemetery nearby having no link with the attack of the North Midland battalions. There is evidence, from the occasional positive identification on headstones, that the remains found after the war were dispersed to at least five distant cemeteries and are buried under 'Unknown Soldier' headstones in concentration plots there. The closest is St Mary's A.D.S. Cemetery on the road running from Vermelles to Hulluch. The other cemeteries are: Loos British Cemetery, on the other side of Loos village; Cabaret Rouge Cemetery, at Souchez; Arras Road

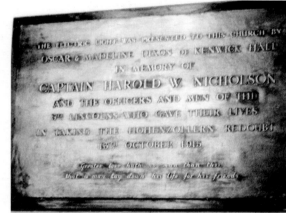

The memorial plaque in the parish church at Legbourne, near Louth, to an officer of the 1/5th Lincolns killed at the Hohenzollern Redoubt. Three of that battalion's four company commanders were killed; none has a known grave. There are numerous memorials like this one throughout the North Midland Division counties.

British Cemetery at Roclincourt and Canadian Cemetery No. 2, at Neuville-St Vaast, on the edge of Vimy Ridge Park. It would not be an exaggeration to say that the remains of the North Midland men who fell in front of the Hohenzollern Redoubt were dispersed to the four winds. It was a far cry from the careful burials in the small 'comrades' cemeteries' and Belgian village churchyards of the earlier trench-holding tours.

There was nothing unique about the sacrifice of the North Midland

The names on the Loos Memorial to the Missing on the walls of Dud Corner Cemetery. The names of the Lincolns are on the left of the small opening of the wall; those of the Liecesters are on the right of the opening. The Sherwood Forester and North and South Stafford panels are on other walls.

The modest First World War memorial for the 46th (North Midland) Division at Vermelles, two miles from the scene of its Hohenzollern Redoubt disaster. Slagheaps of the Loos coalfield area are in the background.

Division at the Hohenzollern Redoubt; many other British divisions on the Western Front experienced such setbacks. There is a small divisional memorial at the side of the road leading out from Vermelles to Hulluch, but the action at the Hohenzollern Redoubt, or even the overall Battle of Loos, does not attract any grand act of remembrance like the sounding of the Last Post each evening at the Menin Gate at Ypres or the crowded ceremonies each First of July to commemorate the opening day of the Battle of the Somme in 1916.

As I wrote in the introduction to this book, 1915 was not a popular year in which to die.

The Battalions, 1916 to 1964

After spending a few weeks recovering in quiet trenches after the Hohenzollern Redoubt disaster, it was decided that the 46th (North Midland) Division should leave the Western Front and be sent to strengthen the defence force on the Suez Canal against possible Turkish attack. The division moved to Marseilles in January 1916 and six battalions – the two Lincolns and all four Staffords – actually sailed and reached Egypt. However the Gallipoli

IN MEMORY OF THE OFFICERS NON-COMMISSIONED OFFICERS AND MEN OF THE 46TH NORTH MIDLAND DIVISION T.A.

The inscription shows that the memorial was erected after the Territorial Force became the Territorial Army in 1921.

Campaign had just ended and a fellow Territorial division just evacuated from the peninsula – the 42nd (East Lancashire) – was sent to the Suez Canal instead. The North Midland battalions sailed back to Marseilles and the division returned to the Western Front.

The next few months were spent in trenches on Vimy Ridge, but then came a move south ready for the next British offensive – the Somme! This time, the division was allocated a place on the opening day of the great attack by thirteen British and five French divisions. The 46th Division's place was on the extreme left of the twenty-mile attack front, taking part with the 56th (London) Division in the diversionary attack on the awkward German salient at Gommecourt. This time, it was the turn of the Staffordshire and the Sherwood Forester Brigades to provide the main part of the division's effort. The results of that infamous day are well known.*

The Germans facing the Staffords and Foresters were ready. It was almost a repeat of the Hohenzollern Redoubt. The attacking waves were mostly cut down in No Man's Land. A few men reached and entered the German

* See the author's *The First Day on the Somme*, in hardback by Pen and Sword Books, and paperback by Penguin Books.

trenches, but none remained alive by nightfall. The division suffered 2,455 casualties, including four battalion commanders killed and one wounded. Major General Montagu-Stuart-Wortley, the divisional commander, was judged not to have pressed the attack hard enough and was sacked.

The North Midland Division had now failed in its first two offensive operations. It had gained the reputation of not being reliable in attack and became a 'line-holder' for the next two years, garrisoning various inactive sectors of the Western Front while other divisions carried out the next three British offensives. It thus missed the Battles of Arras, Passchendaele and Cambrai in 1917 and also, by no more than good fortune, the German offensives in early 1918. This saved the division from further heavy casualties, but the original Territorial character was steadily eroded during two further years of 'trench wastage'. Volunteering for most Territorial battalions was ended in 1917 and was replaced by conscription, and the nominally Territorial North Midland battalions were eventually composed mainly of conscripts and men drafted in from other units. The pre-war Territorial element nearly disappeared; in February 1918, the 1/7th Sherwood Foresters could count only ten men from the thousand who had originally left England in February 1914. It is likely that the other battalions in the division were in the same condition.

The British infantry divisions on the Western Front underwent a major reorganization in February 1918. Their infantry strength had fallen so low due to lack of reinforcements that every brigade, except the Empire ones, was reduced from four battalions to three. The 46th Division thus lost three battalions. However, unlike some other divisions, the three North Midland battalions were not disbanded but were transferred to another division with which they had much in common. This was the 59th Division which had been assembled in England from the Second Line Territorial battalions that had been created at local drill halls from September. Its full title was the 59th (2nd North Midland) Division and it had been serving on the Western Front for the past year. The three battalions sent from the 46th Division were the 1/4th Lincolns, 1/5th North Staffords and 1/7th Sherwood Foresters. On reaching the 59th Division, they were amalgamated with their respective Second Line battalions. There were two benefits from this. First, the South Lincolnshire, Stoke-on-Trent/Potteries and Nottingham City links with the new battalions were maintained; second, the First and Second Line distinctions were abandoned so that the new battalions could now proudly bear their simpler pre-war titles of 4th Lincolns, 5th North Staffords and 7th Sherwood Foresters.

The two North Midland divisions experienced differing fortunes in that last year of the war. The 59th Division was hit hard on 21 March, the first day of the German Spring Offensive – the *Kaiserschlacht*. The division

Men of the North and South Staffords, and probably some Monmouths, on the bank of the St Quentin Canal after successfully breaching the Hindenburg Line there in September 1918. Several men are still wearing the life jackets borrowed for the attack from cross-Channel steamers.

suffered the heaviest casualties of the day, with 807 men killed and most of the remainder being captured in the rapid German advance of that day's fighting. It is ironic that the musketry skills of the few remaining pre-war Territorials in the division were never put to the test. This was the first time they faced Germans attacking in the open, but it was a morning of thick fog and the fighting took place at a range of only a few yards.*

The division was hit hard again a month later in the surprise German attack on the Lys. This time there were no reinforcements available and the division ceased to exist as a fighting force. Most of the battalions were disbanded, including the three that had come from the 46th Division. The 4th Lincolns ceased to exist just three days before Armistice Day.

The 46th Division, the original North Midland Division, by contrast, had missed the German offensives and was still a strong division by the standards of late 1918. It finally had its day of glory when it attacked across the St Quentin Canal and captured a section of the Hindenburg Line in the Allied 'Advance to Victory' Campaign on 29 September. The greater part of this success was due to the initial attack carried out by the Staffordshire Brigade assisted by the 1/1st Monmouths. It was a major victory achieved at a modest cost in casualties. The war ended six weeks later.

Looking at the fortunes of the Boston Territorials who had left England in February 1915, three officers and twenty other ranks had been killed holding the early trenches in Belgium or at the Hohenzollern Redoubt, but only six other ranks died during the remaining three years of the war. This was the result of being in the 46th Division when it was a line-holding division and then in the 59th Division when large numbers of men were taken prisoner in the German attack on that foggy morning in March 1918. It is not known how many of the original battalion remained when the 4th Lincolns disbanded just before the war ended but the numbers, if any, must have been minute; wounds, sickness, transfers to other services and men taken prisoner in 1918 accounted for the remainder.

The only officers from the pre-war Boston Territorials to serve with the battalion after the Hohenzollern Redoubt action were the two Marris brothers. Harold, despite suffering several periods of illness and 'nervous strain', served a total of twenty-one months at the front but eventually succumbed to 'shock and neurasthenia' and was invalided out of the army just before the war ended. Geoffrey Marris also suffered periods of sickness but accumulated two years of active service before being posted to home service in March 1918. Both became captains and it is probable that they shared most of the command of the old Boston 'A' Company after Captain Staniland's successor, Captain Gray, was killed at the Hohenzollern Redoubt. These were honourable service records for the Marris brothers, a comment that can be equally attributed to the handful of unknown warrant

*See the author's The Kaiser's Battle, Penguin Books, for a description of that day's fighting. A young officer of the 4th Lincolns killed on that day was twenty-years-old Second Lieutenant Meaburn Staniland Page whose parents lived in Brigg, but no link between this young officer and the Staniland family from Boston has been established. He has no known grave and his name is recorded on the Arras Memorial to the Missing.

officers, non-commissioned officers and private soldiers who survived death, wounds and sickness and who carried on in the trenches, through all seasons, into the later war years. Major Oliver Cooper did not return to the front after being wounded at the Hohenzollern Redoubt. Lieutenant Ted Beaulah, after a spell in England for 'minor surgery' transferred to the RFC, flew as a pilot on the Western Front, and survived the war. After the war, Harold Marris became Clerk to Holland County Council; Geoffrey Marris returned to farming and Oliver Cooper to his corn merchant's business. Ted Beaulah stayed on in the new RAF and reached the rank of group captain before retiring after the Second World War.

The two original Lincolnshire Territorial battalions were 'reconstituted' in the 1920s and resumed their part-time peacetime roles at the drill halls in the county's towns for the next decade, reverting to the eight-company organization abandoned on the outbreak of the First World War. However in the late 1930s the 5th Battalion, in the north of the county, became a searchlight unit, firstly in the Royal Engineers then in the Royal Artillery. It served in the Second World War as the 46th Searchlight Regiment, Royal Artillery (The Lincolnshire Regiment); the '46th' numbering was almost certainly allocated in memory of its service with the 46th Division in the earlier war.

The 4th Lincolns at Lincoln, Boston and the other towns in the south continued as an infantry battalion until early 1939 when, as part of the doubling in strength of the Territorial Army, it was split into two halves around which two battalions were formed. Initially, these were called the 1/4th and 2/4th Lincolns, but those clumsy First World War titles were not suitable for two battalions of equal status, so they became the 4th and 6th Lincolns. The 4th Battalion retained the Lincoln, Boston, Horncastle and Alford-Spilsby Companies; the 6th took the Grantham, Holbeach, Spalding and Stamford Companies. Conscription was now the policy, service by all, not by the willing volunteers of the early First World War years, and the two battalions were filled up with these 'National Servicemen' and made ready for war. The 4th Lincolns, again with the Boston 'C' Company which had gone to war from the drill hall in Main Ridge in August 1914, fought in Norway in 1940, then went as garrison troops to Iceland before returning to train for the invasion of Normandy. They crossed to France soon after D-Day as part of the 49th (West Riding) Division and fought continuously until V-E Day. The 6th Lincolns were in the 46th (North Midland) Division and took part in the Battle of France in 1940, forming part of the rearguard at Dunkirk, and then fought in the Tunisian and Italian campaigns. The 'West Riding' and 'North Midland' were repeats of the regional subtitles of the same two divisions of the First World War, but the links with those regions were not as close this time.

The original Boston Company title is still preserved above the doorway.

The 4th and 6th Lincolns were amalgamated in 1947 as part of the Royal Lincolnshire Regiment after the 'Royal' prefix was finally granted in 1946, but the end came in the widespread 1964 reorganization when so many county regiments lost their identity. At the time of writing (2002), the Regulars of the Lincolns live on only as 'A' (Lincolnshire) Company of the Royal Anglian Regiment. Territorial infantrymen from the whole county form 'B' (Lincolnshire) Company of the East of England Regiment, Territorial Army, based at Sobraon Barracks at Lincoln. There are no longer Territorial soldiers at any of the drill halls in Lincolnshire. At the drill hall at Boston there is only a Regular Army Recruiting Sergeant and a contingent of the Army Cadet Force that is affiliated to the Parachute Regiment. The Royal Leicestershire and the Sherwood Foresters Regiments experienced broadly similar fates, but a Staffordshire Regiment still exists, although the 'North' and 'South' distinctions have disappeared.

The Drill Hall at Boston to-day, almost unchanged from the building which the local Territorials left for overseas service. Recruiting Sergeant Alan Asker of the Royal Anglians, posing at the author's request, is the only tenuous link with the men of 1914.

The Staniland Family

The Staniland family, once so prominent in Boston, has no descendants living in the town now; one reason for this is the unusually bad fortune its members suffered. For those who have been following its fortunes so far in the book, we can continue their story.

The brothers Second Lieutenant Geoffrey Staniland and Captain Meaburn Staniland were killed in action in Belgium on 14 April and 29 July 1915. A further misfortune struck almost immediately.

Mrs Frances Sophia Staniland was Meaburn Staniland's wife. On his death she became a widow with four small boys; the eldest – twins – were six years old, the youngest less than two years. Mrs Staniland survived her husband by less than six months. On 2 January 1916 she became ill, doubly infected the doctors thought by scarlet fever and German measles. She died five days later. It was popularly thought that the grief of losing her husband and the tragedy of her fatherless little boys lowered her powers of resistance. She was buried at Manby, near Louth, where her father was the rector and where she had spent her childhood. It will be seen that this village churchyard near Louth, in some ways similar to that at Dranoutre, became the final resting place for Meaburn Staniland's family rather than at Wyberton, where his home been, or at Boston the scene of his professional, civic and pre-war Territorial life.

An urgent decision needed to be made about the upbringing of the four small orphan boys. It was a time of great trauma. The first proposal, made at Boston, was that the boys should be split into two pairs and looked after by two of Meaburn Staniland's unmarried sisters but

HEAD OF BOSTON RED CROSS NURSES

Sad Death of Mrs. Meaburn Staniland.

THE LATE MRS. STANILAND AND HER CHILDREN.
The above picture of the fond mother and her young family is intensely pathetic. Less than six months ago the four bonny children were deprived of their father, Capt.

The report of Frances Staniland's death in the Lincolnshire Standard.

the Reverend Hall, Frances's father, at Manby, vetoed this. The boys, he insisted, must be kept together.

Any proposal that the rector and his wife should take the boys in had to be quickly abandoned because the rector's wife, Mrs Fanny Hall, died suddenly on 1 February 1916, less than a month after the death of her daughter. Her death was the result of a possible combination of scarlet fever and an insect bite infection.

The legal guardians of the four boys were, initially, Robert Staniland, Meaburn's father, and Arthur Hall, Meaburn's brother-in-law, still serving with the 1st Dorsets and now a major. Robert Staniland had lost his two sons and a daughter-in-law in nine months; Arthur Hall had lost his mother, a sister, and a brother-in-law and close friends in Meaburn and Geoffrey Staniland. Their problem about who would raise the four boys and whether they could be kept together was solved when a distant cousin and close friend of the boys' late mother came forward and offered to provide a home for them all. This lady, spoken highly of by everyone, was Miss Mary Wright, usually called 'Mamie'. She was a member of a landowning family with estates in North Lincolnshire and South Yorkshire. Robert Staniland died in the early 1920s; Arthur Hall survived the war but then spent many years abroad. Mamie Wright thus became the boys' effective guardian. She belonged to a generation of women many of whose potential husbands were dying in the war. She undoubtedly offered her help for friendship's sake but perhaps she saw the four boys as the only family she might ever have. I have no evidence for this statement; it is only a personal speculation. Mamie Wright and the boys lived at Boston initially, in Skirbeck Road, near their grandfather's home at Hussey House, then at a farm near Ripon where Mamie and her sister produced Wensleydale cheese, and finally at Mamie's parental home at South Anston, near Worksop, though the boys spent most of their time away at Rugby School in later years.

The four boys were twins Robert and John – known as 'Bob' and 'Jack', James – 'Jim', and Meaburn.

The next tragedy occurred in 1932. Jim Staniland, then either eighteen or nineteen years old, had started work for a timber merchant in Boston. One Sunday morning he borrowed his bother Jack's two-seater sports car to drive to South Anston for lunch with Mamie Wright's family. The car crashed on a corner near Newark and Jim was killed. He was buried next to his mother in the churchyard at Manby.

Christopher Stainbank Staniland was the son of Second Lieutenant Geoffrey Staniland who had been killed by shellfire at Pond Farm during the 1/4th Lincolns' first tour of the line in April 1915 and whose grave was the first of the Lincolns' officers to be buried at Dranoutre. He was a cousin of Meaburn and Frances Staniland's sons. He developed a love of fast cars and

The Staniland-Hall group of graves. Jim, killed in a car accident, is buried on the left. There are inscriptions to his brothers Meaburn (the younger) and Jack on the side and back of their mother's grave.

The grave inscription in Manby Churchyard.

for flying; one comment made on his life was that 'he had a passion for speed'. He became a pilot in the RAF as soon as he was old enough to do so. The following years frequently saw him competing in races at the motor-racing circuit at Brooklands, and in his service career he was posted to the RAF's High Speed Flight whose pilots flew in the Schneider Cup Races and he took part in the 1928 Hendon Air Display as an aerobatic pilot. He left the RAF in 1929 to become a test pilot in the aircraft industry, eventually becoming Chief Test Pilot for the Fairey Aviation Company, flying from the company's airfield at Heath Row (now London Heathrow Airport). These years saw Chris Staniland give thrilling demonstrations of new planes that the company hoped to sell to customers and then the testing of new types that the company was making for the Fleet Air Arm for the Second World War. The end came on 26 June 1942. He was flying the second prototype of the Fairey Firefly when, according to the accident report, 'elevator overbalance caused tail plane to collapse at low level dive'; the cockpit hood had been jettisoned 'but no apparent attempt had been made to abandon the aircraft'.*

The plane crashed near Wokingham and Chris Staniland was killed instantly. He was thirty-eight years old. His grave is in St Mary's Churchyard at Keddington, just outside Louth. He shares a headstone with his mother who died in 1949. His mother gave the church a new organ in his memory but the church is no longer in use.

Returning to Meaburn Staniland's sons. The youngest was Major Meaburn Francis Staniland. He was a Territorial officer in the 6th Lincolns in the 46th Division in the Second World War. He fought in Tunisia and in Italy, taking part in the landing at Salerno. A fellow officer in the battalion was Major Ken Barrell; their fathers had served together in the 1/4th Lincolns in Belgium in 1915. Ken was the son of the Lieutenant Colonel Gilbert Barrell from Spalding who had been the 1/4th Lincolns' Commanding Officer when Captain Meaburn Staniland had been killed at Armagh Wood. Major Ken Barrell was killed at Salerno. Major Meaburn Staniland was severely wounded later in the Italian campaign while acting as commander of the Stamford Company. He was hit by one bullet in the mouth and by a second in the shoulder area; this cut a nerve and caused paralysis in one hand. He was officially classified as 80 per cent disabled. After the war he worked for Penguin Books (where he oversaw the design of the cover of my first book, The First Day on the Somme) and then became a second-hand bookshop owner in Stamford. He died in 1992. After his cremation, the urn containing his ashes was buried in the grave of his mother at Manby Churchyard and an inscription to his memory was added on the side of his mother's gravestone.

Major Jack Staniland, like his father, qualified as a solicitor and practised

* Public Record Office, AVIA 5/21, Report W1265.

in the family law firm in Boston, living on London Road, and became a Territorial officer in the 4th Lincolns. He was unmarried. In 1939 he transferred to the newly former 6th Battalion and formed a new company for that battalion at Spilsby and Alford. However on the outbreak of war he returned to the 4th Battalion and became the commander of 'C' Company, exactly the same 'C' Company which his father was commanding at the drill hall in Boston when war broke out in August 1914. After service in Norway, where he was wounded, and in Iceland, he took the Boston Company to Normandy just after D-Day. During a period when the battle became bogged down at the end of June, Major Staniland took out a patrol one misty night to establish the exact locations of the German positions facing the company, not normally a company commander's task. At an intermediate point, he ordered the men with him to stand fast while he went on alone. He encountered the Germans and was fired upon. He dashed back through the mist. One of his men challenged the figure approaching through the mist but Jack Staniland either did not hear – he was slightly deaf – or he was out of breath, and he did not respond. One of his men, a recent reinforcement, fired. Jack Staniland was killed instantly. So, father and son both died, not in actual fighting, one because of the careless lighting of a match, and one in this tragic accident. The unfortunate soldier who fired the fatal shot was killed the following day. Jack Staniland's grave is now in Plot 5, Row B of Manvieu War Cemetery in Normandy. A tribute to him was added on the

A second commander of the Boston Territorials killed in a second war.

rear of his mother's gravestone at Manby, with the letters TD – Territorial Decoration – added after his name. He actually died a few days before the automatic award of that decoration and his twin brother wrote to the War Office asking if the date of the award could be brought forward. The exact outcome of the correspondence has been forgotten, but the family added the letters just the same, feeling that the spirit of the posthumous 'award' was merited.

The remaining son of Meaburn and Frances Staniland was Robert, or 'Bob', the younger of the twins by a few minutes. He had gone into farming, in Berkshire, before the Second World War and was thus in a reserved occupation, but he joined the Local Defence Volunteers (the forerunners of the Home Guard) on the first day of its existence in 1940. He was still alive and very helpful at the time of this book's preparation, aged ninety-two and living in Essex, but very regrettably he died before publication, leaving a widow and two sons and two daughters who are the only direct descendants in their generation of the First World War Captain Meaburn Staniland. They are continuing the use of the Meaburn Christian name in places as far away as New Zealand. The three sisters of Meaburn Staniland survived him for many years, living at various places in and around Boston, but the only one to marry did so at a mature age and had no children.

The LINDENHOEK House Name

Our story is nearly finished. Lance Corporal William Kent recovered from his attack of enteric fever but did not return to his battalion and was transferred to the RFC in a ground service capacity. He survived the war without mishap, returned to Boston and resumed his place in the family monumental mason's business. He had been very friendly with a young local lady, Miss Ottoline Mowbray – 'Ottie' to her friends, a farmer's daughter from Sibsey, but they had decided not to become engaged while the war lasted; they were married soon after it ended. After living in various homes in the next ten years, they had a new house built next to the business premises near Boston Cemetery in Horncastle Road. William Kent decided to call it LINDENHOEK after that meeting place with Captain Staniland's body in 1915.

William Kent did not achieve old age but died of a heart attack suddenly in 1946. It was thought that his heart might have been weakened by the enteric fever that had sent him home from the Western Front soon after Captain Staniland's death. William Kent's widow survived him by thirty-five years! His son, Tom, with his wife, Jane, moved into LINDENHOEK when they married in 1955, but the business and the house was sold in 1990. When Tom and Jane Kent moved to a smaller house closer to the town centre in Boston, they took the LINDENHOEK nameplate with them. Tom died in 1997 but Jane still lives there, a good friend of my wife. When I called to collect my wife there one afternoon in December 2001, I casually asked, 'Jane. Why is your house called LINDENHOEK?'

PART FIVE
The 1915 Sectors Today

After the North Midland battalions left Belgium early in October 1915, they were followed by a succession of other units over the next three years. These experienced long, relatively quiet, periods of trench holding, or shorter, violent, periods of battle. There remains little to see of the trenches the Territorials occupied in 1915 and the maps earlier in the book will show the reader/visitor roughly where the front line was in 1915. There are no known unit or personal memorials in Belgium to any part of the North Midland Division or to any of its members, unless I have made a mistake and missed something.

However there are the graves of nearly 700 of the 917 men of the infantry battalions who died there in 1915 in at least twenty-five Commonwealth War Graves Commission cemeteries or village churchyards. Some of the cemeteries are still the small wartime burial plots made at that time and not substantially added to later; a visit to them is very evocative. Even in those cemeteries that became larger as the war years ran by or were added to by the post-war closure of small cemeteries or the clearance of graves from the battlefields, it is possible to find the rows that were once the original 1915 burials; they usually form Plot 1 in a current cemetery plan and the notes in the following pages will direct you to them. It is important to remember two things in the enlarged cemeteries. Unless his body was lost at the time, nearly

Ruined Ypres immediately after the war – the last city in the country for which Britain had gone to war in 1914 not to have been captured by the Germans.

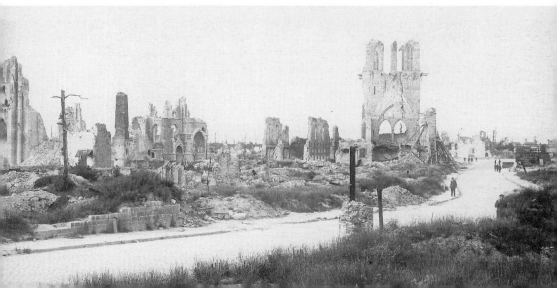

every North Midland man who died in the trenches in 1915 was buried by his own friends in a small cemetery. The second aspect of the large cemeteries is the realization of the extent of the long agony of the BEF, particularly on the Ypres Salient. During the next three years, the casualty list grew, either in the great battles fought there or through the mounting cost of routine trench holding. The Germans repeatedly tried to break the British resolve to hold the line in front of Ypres – the last city in the country for which Britain had gone to war in 1914 not to have been captured by the Germans.

The areas will be described in the order in which the North Midland Division was located in its six months in Belgium. May I remind the reader that I will continue to use the French village names used by the soldiers in the First World War but I will again add the modern Flemish usage in brackets if there is a wide variation between old and new forms. It is appreciated that many other cemeteries and memorials of many kinds are to be found in these areas, but this little touring description is only to those places that are relevant to the sojourn of the Territorials from the North Midland counties here in that spring and summer of 1915.

You will be travelling in areas well off the popular battlefield touring routes. In two-and-a-half days of research and photography, mostly over a September weekend of reasonable weather, my wife and I only encountered one British vehicle – a Landrover at Spanbroekmolen, one place that is on the regular tour routes. If you follow my tour, you will be honouring the memory of many British soldiers whose graves are seldom visited.

Under the Messines Ridge

This was the first sector held by the North Midland Division in April 1915 after its battalions had been given an introduction to trench conditions by more experienced units. The battalions were here for three months, always in trenches overlooked by the Germans on the higher ground, but always with quiet villages in the rear to which they could return to rest every four days. The North Staffords and South Staffords had held the south of the division's frontage, the Lincolnshire-Leicestershire Brigade the centre and the Sherwood Foresters the north. The twelve battalions had been split into pairs, with one battalion in the line and the other resting.

The whole sector remained seemingly quiet for nearly two years after the North Midland Division departed. But the British were making long-term plans. A major tunnelling effort commenced at the end of 1915 and at 3.10am on 7 June 1917, nineteen mines containing 390 tons of explosive were blown under the German trenches on a nine-mile frontage. Twelve divisions of General Plumer's Second Army then swept through the shattered German line and captured the entire Messines Ridge the same day. Eight of these mines were on the front held earlier by the North Midland Division: a group of three at Kruisstraathoek on the left boundary of the Staffordshire Brigade, one each at Spanbroekmolen and near Peckham Corner on the Lincolnshire-Leicestershire frontage and one at Maedelstede Farm, and two at Petit Bois on the Sherwood Foresters' front.

The craters of all but one of those eight mines remain to mark the German line faced by the North Midland battalions two years earlier, only one of the Kruisstraathoek group has been filled in. All are filled with water and some belong to angling clubs. The tree-lined one at Spanbroekmolen has been designated 'The Pool of Peace' and presented to the Toc H organization that was born at Poperinghe in 1915. Visitors can stand at the gateway there and realize what an advantage the Germans had in 1915 looking down on the Lincolns' and Leicesters' trenches just 200 yards away.

The Germans took more than equal revenge in 1918. They mounted a series of massive attacks that spring to try to break the Allies before the Americans could arrive on the Western Front in strength. The last of these blows – known as The Battle of the Lys – fell on a fifteen-mile front from Neuve-Chapelle in the south, as far as Kemmel. Armentières and Bailleul were lost; the Messines Ridge was lost; Kemmel and its great hill were lost; Ypres was nearly outflanked. However a desperate, mainly British, defence just held and one of the most serious crises of the war – though one of the least covered in popular military history – passed. 'Demarcation stones' at various roadsides mark the limit of the German advance. It will be shown, a few pages hence, that a battalion which had once been made up of pre-war Territorials from South Lincolnshire played a part in that fighting.

Most of the local villages were left in ruins but little is known of the effects of the Battle of the Lys on the 1915 cemeteries. Some may have suffered in the fighting, but the location of every grave had been recorded and those cemeteries selected for permanent retention after the war and which we visit now, at least in this area, are the genuine original ones.

The armies departed after the war and the local people returned to rebuild their homes and reclaim their land. No substantial development has taken place and no motorways built in the intervening years and the area retains its quiet rural appearance. It is now known as the Heuvelland, a word meaning 'hilly country'. It is a popular area for leisure pursuits being easily accessible from Ypres, Armentières, and other towns in northern France over the nearby border. There are plenty of small hotels and restaurants. Heuvelland is the product of a comparatively recent local government reorganization. Eight parishes – de Clitte (now Klijte), Kemmel, Locre (Loker), Dranoutre, Neuve Eglise (Nieuwkerke), Westoutre, Wulverghem (Wulvergem) and Wyschaete (Wijtschate) – all lost their burgermeisters and parish clerks and the whole district is now administered by one

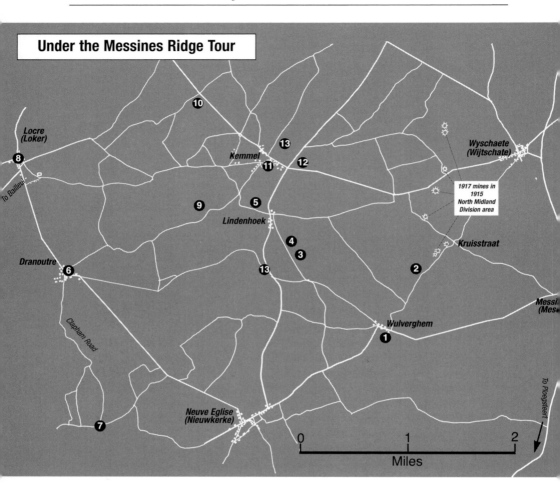

burgermeister and his staff with headquarters in the chateau at Kemmel.
It will be convenient for this little tour to proceed from south to north.

Neuve Eglise and Wulverghem were villages that hosted the Staffordshire battalions when they were out of the line but their churchyards were not used extensively for burials. There are only six graves of mixed ranks at Neuve Eglise and five at Wulverghem, mainly very early burials or 'died of wounds'.

The 1/5th and 1/6th South Staffords quickly decided to take their fatal trench casualties to a new field cemetery which is now St Quentin Cabaret Military Cemetery ❶. It was close by the St Quentin inn just south of Wulverghem which was being used as a battalion HQ. Sixteen men of each battalion were eventually buried there. Their graves are now to be found in Rows G, F and E, just inside this attractive triangular-shaped cemetery. It is believed that the few graves in Row G that pre-date those of the Staffords were brought in after the war. The cemetery continued to be used by front line units for the next three years and now contains 460 graves. The house nearby may stand on the site of the old inn.

The two North Staffordshire battalions decided to use R. E. Farm Cemetery ❷, a small cemetery already established between the farm of that name and Shell Farm. The cemetery was less than half a mile from the German line but was on a slight downward slope and tucked in behind Shell Farm. The 1/5th Battalion buried nine men and the 1/6th nineteen in rows that are now in the far right corner of what is still only a small cemetery of 179 graves.

North and South Staffordshire graves at R.E. Farm Cemetery. Part of Shell Farm can be seen on the right.

The Lincolnshire and Leicestershire battalions in the centre of the divisional front initially established two new field cemeteries by the side of a lane a mile and a half behind the front on either side of Packhorse Farm. The cemetery of the 1/5th Lincolns and 1/4th Leicesters was near a roadside shrine and so became Packhorse Farm Shrine Cemetery ❸. I have a great affection for this simple little cemetery containing the trench dead of Grimsby and the north of Lincolnshire and those from the city of Leicester from the whole of their battalions' three months of service on this front. The two battalions even had their own plots. Near the entrance, the Leicesters have three officers and twenty-four other ranks in three rows; the Lincolns buried twenty-seven men – no officers died – in three rows further back near the Cross of Sacrifice. Among the Lincolns are buried a Royal Engineers' sapper and a Royal Army Medical Corps' private, both members of the North Midland Division. The Leicesters buried with their men two Durham Light Infantry men and one from the Rifle Brigade who were killed when parties from their battalions in the 14th (Light) Division were undergoing trench instruction with the Leicesters. No graves were added after the two battalions moved away and none was removed after the war. This remains the best preserved of those little cemeteries which the North

Midland Division made in 1915.

Only 200 yards away, on the other side of the farm, was Packhorse Farm Cemetery ❹ where the 1/4th Lincolns and the 1/5th Leicesters started to

bury their dead. They had only buried seven and nine men respectively when the battalions were moved slightly north and started using a different cemetery. The little group of sixteen graves was thus left there until after the war when the Army Graves Service reburied the remains elsewhere.

The next burial place moving north is Lindenhoek Chalet Military Cemetery ❺ near the chalet that various battalions used as their HQ. There were only five graves here when the 1/5th and 1/7th Sherwood Foresters arrived. Those five graves are the Suffolks and Londons, from the 28th Division, just inside the entrance on the right. The Sherwood Foresters – men from the cities of Derby and Nottingham – added fifteen of their men before being moved away from this area in May. They were replaced by the 1/4th Lincolns and 1/5th Leicesters who continued their burials with a further sixteen graves to form the four rows now marked A to D. The cemetery continued to be used until October 1917 at which time there were about 250 graves, all in the rows near the lane. The cemetery was enlarged after the war with the addition of 130 graves moved from other

The original 1/5th Lincolns and 1/4th Leicesters graves in Packhorse Farm Shrine Cemetery, not easy to photograph well because the headstones face away from the best vantage point and because the two battalion plots (Leicesters in the foreground and Lincolns further away) have empty space between them. The farm building on the left is part of Packhorse Farm.

places; they form the thirteen shorter rows away from the lane. Among these were the sixteen 1/4th Lincolns' and 1/5th Leicesters graves from Packhorse Farm Cemetery; they are in Plot 2, Rows H, J and L. The cemetery has an imaginative and attractive boundary at the lane side, but the additions later in the war and afterwards have robbed it of the intimate character it must have had in 1915, particularly in that the two groups of Lincolns' and Leicesters' graves could not be reunited.

The nearby hamlet of Lindenhoek is so small that there is not even a name sign on any of its approach roads. The rendezvous between Lance Corporal Kent and the transport bringing Captain Staniland's body from Armagh Wood was presumably either at the crossroads in the hamlet or at the chalet by the cemetery. To drive from Lindenhoek to Dranoutre, through the narrow lanes across the lower slopes of Mont Kemmel, is a reminder of what a long journey it was to bring Meaburn Staniland's body to Dranoutre, particularly if the journey was made with horse transport.

Nearly all the available ground in the Dranoutre Churchyard ❻ had been filled with earlier British burials before the 1/4th Lincolns started

Lindenhoek Chalet Military Cemetery. The original Sherwood Forester and 1/4th Lincolns and 1/5th Leicesters graves are by the entrance; the Lincolns and Leicesters graves brought from Packhorse Farm after the war are close to the far right corner.

The Commonwealth War Graves Commission cemetery sign is the only marker for the crossroads and few houses at Lindenhoek.

The lines of graves started by the 1/4th Lincolns at the side of Dranoutre Churchyard for their officers. The grave of Second Lieutenant Geoffrey Staniland is at the front. When the body of his brother, Captain Meaburn Staniland, was brought to be buried near him three months later, the nearest available space was the third one from the end.

using the village in April 1915, with eighty-one graves in two plots to the left of and in front of the church. Nineteen of these graves were removed after the war because of overcrowding. The row of head-to-foot graves that the Lincolns started when Second Lieutenant Geoffrey Staniland was killed can easily be found on the right of the church, with their commanding officer, Lieutenant Colonel Jessop in Grave No. 5 and that of Captain Staniland way back in No.15, more than fifty yards from his brother. As soon as this row was full, a new location for burials – Dranoutre Military Cemetery – was started in open ground just west of the village. It now has 461 graves.

If I may be permitted a small diversion from our First World War story, a description of two memorials with interesting aspects in the left front corner of the churchyard can be added. The village's own war memorial has carved into it and painted in bright colours the symbol of Flemish Nationalism:

A
V V K
V

Alles Voor Vlaanderen, Vlaanderen Voor Kristus – All For Flanders, Flanders For Christ. Close by is a mock Spitfire tail fin with the inscription '*de Hemptinne, 5 Mei 1942*'. Flight Lieutenant (or Captain in the Belgian Air Force) Baudouin de Hemptinne was the son of an industrialist from Ghent (now Gand); his mother was a baroness. He had escaped to England after the fall of his own country in 1940 and become a fighter pilot in the RAF, taking part in the Battle of Britain. In May 1942 he was in 122 Squadron flying from Hornchuch, providing escort for six Boston light bombers attacking a target at Lille. This was known as a 'Circus' operation – a small bomber force with a large fighter escort hoping to draw up the Luftwaffe into action. There was an air battle above this area and at least five Spitfires were shot down – four from 122 Squadron and one from 313 (Czech) Squadron. A brass plate on the base of the de Hemptinne memorial dedicates it to the 'dead pilots of Circus 157' and gives the names of four who died – de Hemptinne and Sergeant Karel Pavlik (of the Czech squadron) who crashed in the parish of Dranoutre, Flight Sergeant 'Sidney' Jones (actually Stacey

The village war memorial and Flight Lieutenant de Hemptinne's Spitfire 'tailplane' at Dranoutre; the wooded slopes of Mont Kemmel can be seen in the background.

Douglas Jones) who fell near Poperinghe, and a Canadian, Sergeant Roland Ribout, at Neuve Eglise. The fifth pilot, Squadron Leader Fajte, another Czech but flying with 122 Squadron, evaded capture and returned to England. The four dead pilots were reburied after the war in Ypres Town Cemetery Extension (Plot 4, Row A) but the remains of de Hemptinne were later transferred to a Belgian Air Force plot in Brussels City Cemetery at Evere where 163 Belgian airmen who were killed in the Second World War are buried or have memorial stones if they have no known grave. A building in the Belgian Air Force base at Gavere, near Ghent, is dedicated to de Hemptinne.

Another diversion from events of 1915, but a more relevant one, is

Crucifix Hill ❼ which is only a mile and a half south of Dranoutre, down a lane which the soldiers called Clapham Road. It is said that Marshal Foch came here to pray and meditate at the crucifix whenever he was in this area. The reader will remember that the 1/4th Lincolns were amalgamated with the 2/4th Lincolns in the February 1918 reorganization to become, simply, the 4th Lincolns as in pre-war days and were transferred to the 59th (2nd North Midland) Division. When the Germans swept through this area in April 1918, it was the 4th Lincolns who unsuccessfully attempted to hold them on Crucifix Hill, losing about half of their men as casualties in doing so. There may have been a few Territorials from 1915 who remembered their rest days at Dranoutre three years earlier. I have estimated that, if there were any such pre-war men present on Crucifix Hill that day, it was the first occasion in the war on which they were able to use their pre-war marksmanship skills against enemy troops advancing in clear daylight. There is still a crucifix on the hill, but no other sign of that forgotten little battle from a year of so many forgotten battles.

In 1915, Locre (Loker) ❽ was a village safely tucked out of German sight behind Mount Kemmel. Not only was it used by the Sherwood Forester battalions and then the 1/4th Lincolns and 1/5th Leicesters as a rest village but it was also the location of an Advanced Dressing Station. There are two substantial British plots in the churchyard containing 215 graves. There are none from the Lincolns and Leicesters but thirteen are from the Sherwood

Foresters, representing all four battalions in their brigade. Most are in Plot 2, Rows A and B, with one grave in Row F, at the south side of the church. It is probable that most of the Sherwood Foresters were 'died of wounds' because Locre was not the normal burial place for their trench deaths.

Kemmel is the main village of the area. A superb view can be had on a fine day from the tower alongside the Belvedere restaurant on the top of Mont Kemmel ❾ of the surrounding villages, of the Messines Ridge, and as far as the city of Armentières to the south. There is a Demarcation Stone ❿ on the road behind the hill. It marks the limit of the German advance here after they drove French troops off Mont Kemmel in the culmination of the Battle of the Lys in April 1918. The stone has a French pattern helmet on top and piece of equipment on the side to show that this had been a French-held sector at that time, although British units were quickly brought in to prevent a further German advance outflanking Ypres.

In the main village there are several more cafés and restaurants; the one called Het Labyrint has an interesting collection of old local artefacts – civil and religious, not military – and is as good as many a museum.

The units fighting around Messines used several spaces in Kemmel Churchyard ⓫ to bury their dead between October 1914 and March 1915. There was no room left when the Sherwood Foresters came to Kemmel but those early graves are worth a visit, particularly if you would like to see some the comparatively rare cavalry regiment badges on headstones from the 2nd Cavalry Division when it was fighting to hold the Messines Ridge in 1914. A sad little grave with a white headstone in the plot of children's graves is for Ingrid MacDonald, more than likely a Commonwealth War Graves Commission gardener's daughter who died in 1955, aged only three months.

Just outside Kemmel, on the main road down from Ypres, is a luxury restaurant – the Richelieu – which stands on the site of The Doctor's House ⓬ where Lieutenant Colonel Jessop of the 1/4th Lincolns and the two horse holders of the 1/5th Leicesters were killed in June 1915. The original house was so badly damaged in the war that it had to be rebuilt. The local doctor,

The Doctor's House at Kemmel, now a restaurant.

Dr Ruypens, returned to his practice until he retired in 1930 but the building remained the home of other local doctors until 1983 when it became a restaurant.

When the battalions of the Sherwood Forester Brigade came to Kemmel, they found that earlier units had started a small burial plot in the grounds of the local chateau; it is now Kemmel Chateau Military Cemetery ⓭ All four Sherwood Forester battalions used this for their burials, each battalion usually keeping as far as possible to its own row. This cemetery does not have plots, merely very long rows. All but one of the Sherwood Forester graves are now to be found from the middle onwards of Row A (mainly 1/7th Battalion from Nottingham City), Row C (1/5th Battalion, Derby City), and Rows D and E, all on the right of the cemetery. Some of the Sherwood Forester graves have later burials placed among them, but Row E contains an impressive, continuous line of sixty-three Forester headstones,

Long rows of Sherwood Foresters graves in Kemmel Chateau Military Cemetery. These are Rows D and E which contain 88 graves from the 1/6th and 1/8th Battalions.

all of the 1/6th and 1/8th Battalions from the country towns of Derbyshire and Nottinghamshire respectively. The Sherwood Forester Brigade suffered the highest number of fatal casualties when the North Midland Division held this sector for three months, losing six officers and 145 other ranks; 113 of those men are buried here. All six of the dead officers are buried among their men.

The cemetery continued to be used throughout the war and now contains over 1,100 First World War graves as well as the only Second World War burials in this area – just twenty-one British graves in a row just inside the entrance. Be careful when driving to this cemetery. It appears on a map to be near the main road from Ypres, but the only access is from the main part of the village.

The Ypres Salient

It will be more difficult to describe the area in which the North Midland Division found itself in the months of July to September 1915, among those woods – Zouave, Sanctuary and Armagh – and then down past Mount Sorrel, Hill 60, The Dump and The Bluff until the front line reached the debris chocked Ypres-Comines Canal. Several factors are responsible for the difficulty. First, and most important, are the effects on the wartime cemeteries of the fighting in the woods area in 1916. Then there was the switch of the Sherwood Forester Brigade from the division's left flank to the south after the 'Action at Hooge', so that there is an extra brigade sector to be described. Next, there were no quiet rest villages in the immediate rear; distant Ouderdom has nothing to contribute to our tour. Instead, the introduction of the brigade reserve positions brings in a new aspect. So, instead of a simple journey through a succession of cemeteries and rest villages, we will now be looking at a contrasting area.

The events of 1916 have already been described. It needs merely to be restated that the Germans attacked the Canadian-held line in the woods, drove the Canadians back for a mile and then the Canadians counterattacked and regained most of the lost ground, all within a week. Up to five small cemeteries just behind the original front line that had been used by the North Midland battalions the previous year were so severely damaged that they could not be re-established after the war. The following year, 1917, saw the mounting of the great British offensive that ran from the end of July to mid-November. The area in which the North Midland Division held trenches in 1915 formed the southern flank of the opening attack and the British advance moved the fighting line steadily away from it

Then in 1918 came an event that the British soldiers of earlier years would have found unbelievable. The BEF was so short of men after stemming the German spring offensives that it was forced to shorten its line. A huge withdrawal took place in front of Ypres. All the ground held in 1914, 1915 and 1916, and taken at such cost in 1917, right up to Passchendaele nearly six miles away, was relinquished and the divisions fell back to a new line just outside Ypres. This voluntary withdrawal, together with the earlier gains in the Kemmel-Messines area in the Battle of the Lys in April of that year, meant that every trench maintained and defended by the North Midland battalions on both of its 1915 sectors, and every village in which they had rested, except Ouderdom, passed into German hands. However the balance of strength on the Western Front changed in favour of the Allies and the Germans were steadily pushed out of the whole area in the final weeks of the war – until 1940.

For the description of this area as it is today, it will be best to start in that tortured area of woods held by the Sherwood Forester and Lincolnshire-Leicestershire Brigades in 1915. The tour should start in Maple Avenue (Canadalaan to the Belgians), making for Sanctuary Wood. The open ground to the left, on part of which can be seen the impressive Hooge Crater Cemetery, is where the Sherwood Foresters became involved in the 'Action at Hooge' at the end of July 1915. Continuing on, the road bends, first right and then left; that was to skirt the wartime remains of Zouave Wood when the road was made, but that wood has now disappeared. You soon come to

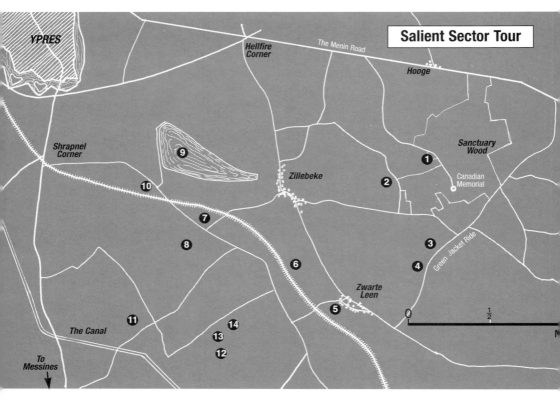

Sanctuary Wood Cemetery ❶ about which there is much to write.

Several major decisions were made about this area after the war. A new road – Maple Avenue – needed to be made to provide access to a large monument which the Canadians were going to build on Tor Top to commemorate the fighting in June 1916. A second decision was taken by the Army Graves Service that no attempt would be made to restore most of the battered cemeteries in the woods area, as many of the graves in them as possible would be recovered and concentrated into one large cemetery to be created alongside the road to the proposed Canadian memorial, using the remains of the one wartime cemetery there to be spared as its nucleus. The graves were moved and the Imperial War Graves Commission thus created the Sanctuary Wood Cemetery which many of us have visited. The search for graves among the old cemeteries and the concentration of them into the new plots must have been very difficult; It took five years to complete the work, from 1927 until 1932.

The only original graves of the cemetery are those at the back in Plot 1 where there are just forty-nine scattered headstones, thirty-one of which are unidentified. Two of the identified ones are of particular interest. Lieutenant Gilbert Talbot, son of a bishop according to his entry in the cemetery register, was the young Rifle Brigade officer killed in the 'Action at Hooge' the day after Meaburn Staniland was killed at Armagh Wood and in whose memory Talbot House at Poperinghe and the Toc H organization are named. An interesting note in the cemetery register's introduction shows that Talbot's brother, Revd. Neville Talbot, an army chaplain, made

Sanctuary Wood Cemetery.

the first list of graves for the original cemetery; that would have made for interesting reading but it has not survived. Unfortunately Gilbert Talbot's headstone is a poor photographic prospect because it is badly weathered and faces away from the sun. The ravages of time are making it increasingly difficult to photograph some of the First World War headstones.

The second grave of interest here is that of Private Aaron Sisson of the city of Nottingham's pre-war Territorial battalion. He is the only one of approximately 200 men of the Sherwood Forester and Lincolnshire-Leicestershire Brigades to have died in the trenches of the woods area to have an identifiable grave in its original position – a stark example of how drastic were the results of the 1916 fighting and the post-war movement of graves.

Four new plots were made after the war, arranged in an attractive fan shape between the old cemetery and the new road. These concentration plots contain graves from the abandoned cemeteries in the woods area as well as others from many other places in a wider area of the Ypres Salient for which burial space needed to be found. There are nearly 2,000 graves, of which almost 70 per cent are unidentified. Among these new plots can be found four groups of the North Midland graves that were moved:

1. Rows D, E and F in Plot 2, on the right, has twenty-two named graves of the 1/7th and 1/8th Sherwood Foresters and fourteen known to be Sherwood Foresters but with no individual identification. Many of these men were casualties from the 'Action at Hooge'.

2. Row M at the rear of the same plot has nine graves of the Lincolns, eight of them from the 1/4th Battalion and one from the 1/5th.

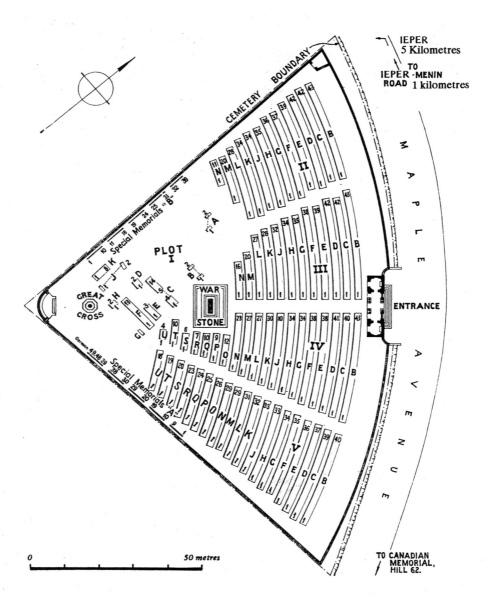

The plan of Sanctuary Wood Cemetery. The scattered graves of Plot 1 between the
Great Cross and the War Stone are all that remains of the original cemetery here.
The four post-war concentration plots contain many graves recovered from up to
four other wartime cemeteries in and around Sanctuary and Armagh Woods
battered during the 1916 fighting.

3. Rows P to T of Plot 4 contain thirty-four graves from the Lincolnshire-Leicestershire Brigade.
4. Row C of Plot 5 has seven 1/5th Sherwood Forester graves and three from the Staffordshires.

Many of these graves, even though fully identified with a dead soldier's name, are marked 'BURIED NEAR THIS SPOT'. All this shows that the contents of at least four damaged cemeteries were moved here in some confusion. Furthermore, a few identified graves from the two brigades can be found in concentration plots in three more distant cemeteries – Hooge Crater, Bedford House and Ypres Reservoir, which is on the north edge of Ypres. There are many 'Unknown Lincolnshire, Leicestershire or Sherwood Forester' graves within the cemetery, further evidence that the remains of so many of the men of the two North Midland brigades who were killed holding trenches in Zouave, Sanctuary and Armagh Woods are now widely scattered and lost to human knowledge.

We can leave this long discourse at Sanctuary Wood Cemetery and complete our journey down the lane. There can be few visitors to the Ypres Salient who have not visited the café here with its museum and trenches. The trenches are genuine but they are not of 1915; it is the new line that the Canadians made after their counterattack in June 1916. At the end of the lane – it is a dead end – is the impressive Canadian memorial and park on Tor Top. I always take visitors to the right-hand viewing point to show them Maple Copse half a mile away across the fields and the open ground as far

Lincolns and Leicesters graves in the rear of Plot 4, many only known to be buried nearby.

as the outskirts of Ypres which is two miles away. It was to deny the German artillery observers the advantages of that view that the North Midland battalions had to defend their trenches in 1915 and for which the Canadians had to fight so hard in 1916. The 1916 fighting left the crest of Tor Top in No Man's Land for the following twelve months, the Canadian effort was not wasted.

(The visitor should not be confused by the erroneous inscription on the Canadian memorial stone which states: HERE AT MOUNT SORREL; it should read: HERE AND AT MOUNT SORREL).

One must return to the Menin Road to reach Maple Copse Cemetery ❷. The present copse is not in the same position as the wartime one; it was on the other side of the cemetery at that time. It was a useful support position, providing cover for troops close to the front and also for forward medical units. The cemetery was used both for the burials of fatal trench casualties and for men who died of wounds here. It is likely that the 1/6th Sherwood Foresters used it for their men killed in the trenches; it is the only Forester battalion not to have graves in Sanctuary Wood Cemetery. This cemetery was also affected by the 1916 fighting but it was decided to retain it after the war, although it was found that only twenty-eight of the original 256 graves could be accurately located. Most of the headstones are in symbolical rows and those with names on them are marked KNOWN TO BE BURIED IN THIS CEMETERY. The six

The beautiful Maple Copse Cemetery with its orderly rows of headstones, but most of the headstones are only symbolical.

Sherwood Forester headstones are widely separated in Rows B, E, G and J. Most of the burials were by units who came here after the departure of the North Midland Division, the majority being the 142 Canadians buried here. Perhaps the Canadian representative on the Imperial War Graves Commission insisted that the cemetery should be preserved. It was well worth saving; it is a most attractive spot.

From Maple Copse it is possible to drive over Observatory Ridge; the lane across it looks straight at the German line. A right turn at the T-junction

The field alongside Green Jacket Ride (the lane on the left) in which the British front line near the edge of Armagh Wood was in 1915. Mount Sorrel is in the trees ahead; the edge of Armagh Wood has receded to the right. Captain Staniland was killed and Sergeant Crick was fatally wounded somewhere within 150 yards of the place from where the photograph was taken.

brings you to that part of Green Jacket Drive ❸ where it runs right through the middle of the No Man's Land which separated the trenches held so often by the 1/4th Lincolns and the 1/5th Leicesters and the Germans. The British front line was less than a hundred yards back from the road, just outside the edge of Armagh Wood. Most of the wood has disappeared now. The German line was a similar distance the other side of Green Jacket Drive, just outside Shrewsbury Forest which is still there. The section of trench in which Captain Staniland was killed and where my uncle was fatally wounded was between a small farm close to the west side of the lane and Mount Sorrel. The trench used by the Lincolns and Leicesters was is in a grass field that has the typical uneven appearance of ground that has never been ploughed since the First World War. I thought I could even distinguish the line of the trench, but that may have been wishful thinking. Further down the lane, Mount Sorrel ❹ is not immediately obvious because of its partially wooded covering. This was the hill whose original name was 'Mountsorrel', so christened by the 1/5th Leicesters after the home of their commanding officer.

We are about to move out of the 1915 wooded area. A sad aspect of the post-war treatment of the area is that, while many thousands of people visit Sanctuary Wood each year, equally important places like Observatory Ridge, Green Jacket Drive, Armagh Wood and Mount Sorrel are hardly remembered. Perhaps these notes might redress the imbalance a little.

At the hamlet of Zwarte Leen is Hill 60 ❺, its trenches mostly held by the 1/5th North and 1/6th South Staffords. This is on the popular visiting route, deservedly so with its crater, a concrete pill-box which looks two ways, memorials from many wartime events and another friendly local café with a museum.

Larch Wood (Railway Cutting) Cemetery ❻ was about 500 yards behind the British front line at Hill 60. It is the first cemetery in this area that escaped the ravages of the 1916 fighting. The reader may remember the descriptions of how Corporal Charlie Burchnall of the Boston Territorial Company was killed by a whizz-bang and how he was buried by his friends

Larch Wood (Railway Cutting) Cemetery.

'in the little cemetery by the railway line' (see page 59). His grave, and those of two other men from the 1/4th Lincolns killed the same day, are together in Row B of Plot 1 at the far end of the cemetery. My wife, Mary, was impressed by the family inscription on Corporal Burchnall's grave: TO LIVE IN HEARTS WE LEAVE BEHIND IS NOT TO DIE. The other two Lincolns are Privates Albert Goodship and John Curtis, both Lincoln men. Private Goodship's entry in the cemetery register shows that he was an old soldier, having served eight years as a Regular in the Bedfordshire Regiment before the war. The dual name of the cemetery may be because two small cemeteries with different names eventually merged to become one.

The 1/4th Lincolns soon moved to the woods sector and the 1/5th North Staffords and 1/6th South Staffords took over the Hill 60 trenches for many weeks and used this cemetery regularly during that time. The graves of twenty-five North Staffords, men from Stoke-on-Trent and the other Pottery towns, and twenty-one South Staffords, from the Wolverhampton area, are to be found all across the rows at that far end of the cemetery. When the Staffords left at the end of September 1915, there were probably no more than sixty graves in the cemetery; there are now 856.

Zillebeke is the only village in the whole area. Its churchyard has one of the most interesting groups of graves for officers brought back from the battlefield in the early part of the war. Seven of them are from Guards regiments and six from the cavalry, with an emphasis on society families: there are two barons, one lord and an 'Honourable'. At least two headstones have particularly interesting personal inscriptions. The Demarcation Stone ❼ at a road junction outside the village again marks the limit of the German advance in 1918. This time it was not as a result of a German attack but of the voluntary retirement by the BEF to shorten the line in front of Ypres in its manpower crisis after the Spring battles of that year. The helmet and equipment shown are of British types.

Blauwepoort Farm Cemetery ❽ is, to my mind, a little gem. There are basically just three and a half rows of graves representing three divisions.

The gap in the right hand row is where the first burials – French *Chasseurs Alpins* – have been removed to be buried with their comrades elsewhere. On the right and at the top of the centre row are thirty-five graves, nearly all from the 5th Division. After the 1/5th Leicestershire buried one man in the second row, the 1/5th South and 1/6th North Staffords took over the cemetery for the duration of their service here, burying seven and seventeen men respectively in the left hand row, men from the Walsall and

The lovely little Blauwepoort Farm Cemetery.

Burton-on-Trent areas. When the North Midland Division left to go to its first battle at Loos, it was replaced by the depleted battalions of the 9th (Scottish) Division coming to recuperate here after suffering heavy losses in their first battle at Loos. Twenty-three Scots were buried in the long middle row.

The cemetery was not used again and there now remain just eighty graves. One is an artilleryman, the remainder are the infantry of three divisions, one Regular, one Territorial and one New Army whose men had held the front line trenches at and around The Dump a mile away. The men had brought their dead to this farm with blue gates for burial. Blauwepoort Farm alongside the cemetery is now a smart private residence, but it still has blue gates.

Dugouts made in the extensive banks of Zillebeke Lake ❾ (Zillebeekse Vijver) provided one of the main brigade reserve positions used by the North Midland battalions behind the woods area. It can be pleasant to sit in the restaurant or by the lake, but it is difficult to visualize the hundreds of troops who once sheltered here.

The large Railway Dugouts (Transport Farm) Burial Ground ❿ probably has the most attractive layout of any cemetery in this area. The railway embankment, the dugouts in the side of which provided the other main brigade reserve position, and Transport Farm by the road are both immediately obvious. There were only two small groups of graves when the North Midland battalions came here, one in what is now the far left corner near the railway and another in the far right near the farm – two little cemeteries a hundred yards apart. The North Midland battalions used the one by the railway; it only had seventeen graves in it before their first burials. The subsequent graves were mostly of men who died of wounds

Two small cemeteries in 1915, at the distant left by the railway embankment and on the right by Transport Farm, now joined by wartime growth and post-war additions to produce one of the most impressive and attractive cemeteries in this area.

received at the front or those caught by shelling while in brigade reserve here. Twenty-two North Midland men were buried in what are now Rows C and E of Plot 1 – thirteen Lincolns, eight Staffordshires and Lieutenant Tarr, the rugby international from Leicester. In Row E is a communal grave for the seven men of the 1/4th Lincolns, including the two Boston sergeants who were killed at the dugouts by a shell on 2 September.

There were probably no more than sixty graves in the two separate Railway Dugouts and Transport Farm cemeteries when the North Midland Division left; the one combined cemetery now contains nearly 2,500 graves!

*   *   *   *   *

Following the casualties of its battalions at the 'Action at Hooge', the Sherwood Forester Brigade was transferred to a quieter sector in the south, holding trenches between The Dump and The Bluff for the last few weeks of the division's service in Belgium. Those weeks passed without serious loss, except for one bad day on 30 September when the 1/6th Foresters lost most of a platoon killed or wounded by an underground mine explosion. Thirty-one men from the four battalions were buried, mostly in three cemeteries started earlier, as so many others, by the 5th Division. The bodies of eleven victims of the mine explosion were never recovered.

The 1/5th and 1/6th Sherwood Foresters – the two Derbyshire battalions – used Chester Farm Cemetery ⓫, one of two cemeteries near the Palingbeek Nature Reserve on the canal which formed the brigade's southern boundary. The 5th Division had left six rows of graves on the roadside which contained the surprisingly high number of ninety-two from the 2nd Manchesters whose companies had earlier held the trenches at The Bluff for eighty-seven consecutive days. The Sherwood Foresters added the graves of fifteen of their men on the left end of the first three of those rows, four of them being the only victims of the 30 September mine explosion to have their bodies recovered. The exact location of three graves of the 1/5th Sherwood Foresters was later lost and they have 'Special Memorials' along the left wall of the cemetery.

The final part of our tour brings us to three remote cemeteries on the edge of woodland which was in the immediate rear of the front line in 1915. The cemeteries near Zouave, Sanctuary and Armagh Woods which were lost because of the 1915 fighting must have been just like these. There is no road access to any of them and the visitor may be tempted to strike across a field but the best access is along the maintained grass pathway near the Commonwealth War Graves Commission signs at the roadside. A complicated system of pathways in and out of the woodland links the three cemeteries. To see all three is not a journey for the infirm.

The reconstructed Hedge Row Trench Cemetery.

The southernmost of the three is the quaintly named Hedge Row Trench Cemetery **12** where the 1/7th Sherwood Foresters buried eight men. Unfortunately, the cemetery suffered shellfire damage later in the war and the exact positions of all the ninety-six graves could not be guaranteed. The war graves service of any other country would have taken the remains to be concentrated elsewhere but the Imperial War Graves Commission decided to retain it, creating a circle of forty-four of the headstones, with the remaining ones placed in lines around the walls. I try not to wax too lyrical but this is a lovely, peaceful resting place by the wood for what were last casualties of the Territorials from the city of Nottingham during the battalion's service in Belgium. Looking at the cemetery plan before leaving home, I thought it would make an ideal subject for a

photograph but the undue size of the circle and the lack of a good vantage point produced a result which does not do full justice to the beauty of the spot.

The second cemetery, 1st D.C.L.I. Cemetery **13**, was, as its name suggests, created by that Regular battalion of Duke of Cornwall's Light Infantry. It contains no Sherwood Forester graves but its position on the slightly higher ground of the Bluff provides a fine view on a good day across the countryside to Ypres. There are only eighty-nine graves in the cemetery; forty-one of them are of the DCLI.

Finally, Woods Cemetery **14**, was started by the 1st Dorsets and the 1st East Surreys. The 1/8th Sherwood Foresters only needed graves here for four of their dead and they were added to the Dorsets and East Surreys

A view to Ypres from 1st D.C.L.I. Cemetery on part of The Bluff shows how close the Salient line was from the city the BEF prevented the Germans capturing for four years.

in Row A of Plot 1. The cemetery continued to be used for two more years and now has 326 graves in a confusing pattern of plots that had to conform to the shape of the wood's edge.

* * * * *

We have visited the graves of a majority of the thirty-nine officers and 878 other ranks of the Territorial infantry battalions of the 46th (North Midland) Division who died on active service in Belgium from March to October 1915. There are a few more graves of men who died of wounds at various Dressing Stations further behind the front, at the Casualty Clearing Stations at Bailleul and Lijssenthoek, at base hospitals on the coast, or even at hospitals in England. There are still 165 infantrymen of the division – seventy-three Sherwood Foresters, thirty-eight Lincolns, thirty-four Leicesters and twenty Staffords – who have no known graves, but they are not forgotten. Silver bugles blow at the Menin Gate to remind us of them every evening of the year.

They shall not grow old,
  As we that are left grow old.

Age shall not weary them,
  Nor the years condemn.

At the going down of the sun,
  And in the morning
WE WILL REMEMBER THEM

John Pearl, a Second World War
Bomber Command veteran from
Nottingham, gives the Exhortation
at The Last Post Ceremony in
memory of the men with no known
grave of an earlier war.

APPENDIX

The Naming of Lijssenthoek Military Cemetery

At some stage after my Uncle Andrew – Sergeant Crick – died of his wounds in October 1915, his family was informed that his grave was in Remy Siding Cemetery. By 1923, however, when the Imperial War Graves Commission published the cemetery register, the name had been changed to Lijssenthoek Military Cemetery. No trace of a second letter has survived if the family was informed of the change. My mother only knew of Remy Siding Cemetery. Today's Commonwealth War Graves Commission has no record about when the new name came into use.

Many visitors coming to Ypres by road approach the area by leaving the Dunkirk-Lille motorway at Steenvoorde and then driving to Poperinghe along a main road which is the D948 while it is in France and N38 when it enters Belgium at the now unmanned Customs Post just over a mile from Steenvoorde. As they approach Poperinghe, they may spot the Cross of Sacrifice of Lijssenthoek Military Cemetery on the right, behind the buildings of a farm – Remi Farm to the local Belgians, Remy Farm to a Frenchman. To visit the cemetery one must use a series of side lanes. That

Lijssenthoek, or Remi Siding, Cemetery immediately after the war. On the left is part of Remi Farm and in the centre and right the extensive wartime CCS expansions. The main gateway being used at the time is probably between Plots 15 and 16 (XV and XVI on the plan).

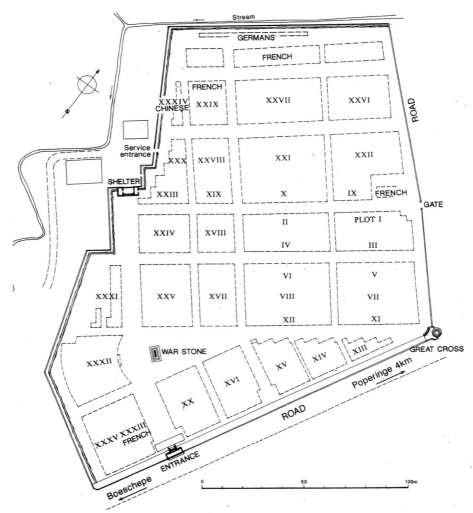

The Commonwealth War Graves Commission plan of Lijssenthoek Military Cemetery.

straight run along the N38 into Poperinghe is along a road that was only built in 1983. Before then, the main road was through Abeele village along a lesser road now marked N333. (The old Customs Post in Abeele village is now a café incorporating many features of its former use interestingly preserved – well worth a visit).

The coming of the First World War to this area found Poperinghe connected to both the Belgian and French railway systems by a line eastwards to Ypres, which soon became unusable because of German shelling, and another line south-westwards into France through Abeele and Godewaersvelde (which British soldiers soon christened 'Gertie wears velvet') to Hazebrouck. This line was not affected by shelling. Poperinghe soon became the Casualty Clearing Station centre for the Ypres front. A Casualty Clearing Station is a British medical unit that has surgeons and nurses and needs to be far enough back from the front to be safe from shellfire and should, ideally have access to a railway line so that those wounded who were fit to travel could be swiftly and comfortably evacuated to the Base Hospitals on the French coast and then on to England. There were cemeteries at each stage for those who died during this process. Poperinghe, initially, was safe from shelling and had a good railway station. Those wounded who died there were buried, firstly, in the Communal Cemetery (only twenty-three British grave), then in what is now Poperinghe Old Military Cemetery which has 450 graves. (The empty grassed space in that cemetery is where about 800 French and Belgian soldiers and nearly 500 Belgian civilians who died in a typhoid epidemic at the end of 1914 were once buried but whose remains have all been reburied elsewhere).

In April 1915, however, after the Second Battle of Ypres brought the Germans closer to Ypres, long-range shells started to fall in Poperinghe and the Casualty Clearing Station presence in the town was reduced. The French had already established one of their equivalents of a Casualty Clearing Station – the *15eme Hôpital d'Evacuation* – at a farm near the railway line half way between Poperinghe and Abeele. The British decided to move most of their Casualty Clearing Station treatment from Poperinghe to the same place. Nos 10 and 17 Casualty Clearing Stations arrived there in June 1915 and remained there for the remainder of the war except for a few weeks in 1918 when the Germans came even closer to Ypres and forced a temporary withdrawal to a safer place.

The farm was a typical Flemish farm and most of the early medical work was carried out in the farm buildings. The owner was a French lady, Madame Bogaert from Hazebrouck. The pre-war tenant was a Belgian, Remi Quaghebeur, but he had died just after the outbreak of war leaving his widowed wife, Marie, and seven children. They remained at the farm for the remainder of the war except for a short period in 1918 when the area briefly came within range of long range German shelling and Marie and the younger children moved temporarily to Watou. The farm had been known locally as Remi Farm but when the French medical unit arrived they used their version – Remy Farm – and the British continued that usage, and so will I for the time being.

It was still early days for the British when my uncle was brought here with his serious abdominal wound in October 1915. There was no British padre.

When Abbé Tiberghien wrote to my grandparents after his death he stated that he had buried Sergeant Crick 'in the little cemetery near our hospital'. As the war progressed and ever-greater battles of Ypres followed, the Remy Farm area was transformed into what was probably the largest Casualty Clearing Station centre on the Western Front. Extensive hutted medical accommodation was erected (on the Poperinghe side of the present-day cemetery) and a new railway siding was laid for the evacuation onwards of wounded who were able to travel – hence the letter to Sergeant Crick's family that his grave was in Remy Siding Cemetery.

Also transformed was Abbé Tiberghien's 'little cemetery'. By the end of the war there were over 9,000 British graves. It was by far the largest British cemetery on or close to the Western Front and the second in size in all Belgium and France. It was only exceeded by the 11,000 men buried at the Base Hospital centre at Etaples. A few isolated graves were brought to Remy Siding just after the war and there are now 9,901 British graves. These include a nurse, Sister Nellie Spindler from Wakefield who was 'killed in action', probably in an air raid, in August 1917 (Plot 1916, Row A), and 883 graves of other nationalities – wounded French soldiers and German prisoners who died here, and a few Chinese labourers who succumbed to sickness or accident. The cemetery was superseded in size only when the tiny battlefield at Tyne Cot near Passchendaele was made into a major concentration cemetery when that battlefield was cleared of graves and unknown bodies. Tyne Cot contains nearly 12,000 graves, so the cemetery at Remy Farm is now the third largest British war cemetery, not only in Belgium and France, but also in the whole world.

Sergeant Crick was one of the earliest of that host of men who suffered and died at Remy Farm. His grave is in the second row of the first plot of British graves to be established. It is close to the small entrance known as the French Gate, the original wartime entrance through which the dead were brought from the farm or the hutted buildings where they had died. There are now thirty-four plots! Nearly all of the graves are of 'trench burials', the bodies having been laid shoulder-to-shoulder in a continuous grave. Only the officers have individual graves in their own rows.

At some stage the cemetery ceased to be known as Remy Siding Cemetery and became Lijssenthoek Military Cemetery; the Imperial War Graves Commission published the first cemetery register under that title in 1923. There were other changes. The Remy Siding railway halt was closed after the war and the entire stretch of line was closed in 1964. For a few years it became a walkers' footpath but then the new road, N38, was constructed in 1964 along the route of the old railway. The new road runs from its junction with the original main road south-east of Abeele, through what was once Abeele Station which was outside the village, past Remi Farm and on to join the ring-road outside Poperinghe. So, if the reader drives along that road from Steenvoorde to Poperinghe, he or she is following for that part of the journey exactly the same route that trains brought so many thousands of British soldiers up to Poperinghe to detrain there to be sent to the Ypres front, and down which not quite so many lucky leave men and wounded travelled.

And just off to one side is Lijssenthoek Military Cemetery, a representation of so much suffering of badly wounded men who failed to survive to make that journey to Blighty. There remain two more comments to be made about the cemetery name. Lijssenthoek is really 'Lysenthoek', an area of scattered farm buildings but with no village centre stretching from the de Leene Estaminet near Poperinghe down to the French frontier near Boeschepe. Lysenthoek is actually part of the municipality of Poperinghe. The 'hoek' part translates as corner so, with the frontier only a mile and a half away, the men and the nurse who were buried at Remy Farm really do lie 'in a corner' of that country for which the British Empire went to war in 1914.

The last point to be made is that the local people do not use the word Lijssenthoek or Lysenthoek for the cemetery. To them it is always the *Remi Kerkhof* – the Remi Cemetery, reverting to the Flemish name for Remy Farm.

The long rows of graves beyond the author's wife standing by Sergeant Crick's grave which is the second grave from the side wall, illustrate the wartime growth of 'the little cemetery' of 1915.

ACKNOWLEDGEMENTS

This book has relied for much of its source material from private individuals and I would like to express my gratitude for the help that has been given by these kind people.

The families of the 1915 Territorial Soldiers. I must thank, above all, the following relations of the men whose story has been told. All have helped without restraint; some elderly members have submitted patiently to repeated questions. They are: Robert Staniland, one of the twin sons of Captain Meaburn Staniland, but who unfortunately died before the book was published; Elizabeth Staniland, widow of Major Meaburn Staniland who was another of Captain Staniland's sons; Rear Admiral Geoffrey Hall, son of Major Arthur Hall; Barbara Pallister, friend of the Staniland and Hall families; Jane Kent, daughter-in-law of Lance Corporal William Kent; Philip Cooper, great nephew of Major Oliver Cooper; Philip Marris, great nephew of Captains Harold and Geoffrey Marris; Tony Beaulah and Bob Isaac, son and nephew respectively of Group Captain Ted Beaulah; my brother, David Middlebrook, nephew of Sergeant Andrew Crick.

Of many other helpers, two people deserve special thanks: my wife, Mary, and my battlefield touring partner, Mike Hodgson. This has been my first attempt at word processing a manuscript and Mary has repeatedly had to come to my rescue, sacrificing much of her spare time in doing so. Mary was also an invaluable companion on a tour of the relevant battlefield areas and her photographic skills can be seen in many of the illustrations in the book. Mike Hodgson has generously allowed the long-term loan of books from his valuable collection of unit histories and other publications, and has acted as my consultant numerous times on the history of Lincolnshire Territorials and on many other subjects.

Other private individuals who have helped in a variety of ways are: Jack Cannon, Maureen Cook, Ann Farmer, Tom Freeston, Philip Hanby, Brian Hayes, Paul Howden, Bill Hunt, Stuart Lowther, Bill Parker and George Wright, all from the Boston area; Melanie and Michael Pocklington of William Kent (Memorials) Ltd, Boston; Cheryl Arnold, Kevin Burton, John Chester, John Gale and George Plowman from Spalding; Colonel F. C. L. Bell, Commanding Officer of the 6th Lincolns in the Second World War, who lives at Chiddingfold in Surrey; John Ellwood from Mareham-le-Fen near Horncastle; Janet and Stuart Farmer from Leicester Tigers Rugby Football Club; Tom Finton from Seacroft near Skegness; Jack Gardiner from Newby near Scarborough; Jim Grundy from Hucknall; Robert Hodgson from Horncastle; John Larder from Boston Spa; Lieutenant Colonel Matt Limb from Grantham; Wynne Smith from West Ayton near Scarborough; Roy Staples from Holbeach and my granddaughters, Alice and Jessica Hamilton-Webb from Cheltenham.

Helpful organisations and official bodies have been: the Air Historical Branch of the Ministry of Defence (Sebastian Cox), the Commonwealth War

Graves Commission (particularly Carol Gamble, also Maria Choules and Peter Stainford), the Imperial War Museum, the *Boston Standard* for granting permission to quote extracts from and reproduce photographs from 1913-1915 issues of the *Lincolnshire Standard*, the Museum of Lincolnshire Life (particularly Rosalind Boyce), the National Rifle Association, the archive staff of the Boston Public Library, and the *Spalding Free Press* for publishing a letter requesting help.

Historians of the North Midland Division regiments who deserve my thanks for various contributions are Captain John Lee of the Royal Lincolnshires, Colonel Anthony Swallow of the Royal Leicestershires, Celia Green of the Monmouthshires, and Major Edward Green and Colour Sergeant Willie Turner of the Staffordshires, also Sergeants Alan Asker and Graham Matthews of the Royal Anglians, Recruiting Sergeants at the Drill Hall in Boston.

In Belgium I was helped by old friends and made many new ones. Every request that I made of the Ieper Tourist Office and Town Museum through Fernand Vanrobaeys and Dominiek Dendooven, and of Johan Vandelanotte at the Heuvelland Tourist Office, was promptly granted. Michel Vansuyt of Ieper, but who was born and brought up near Spanbroekmolen, gave much helpful advice from his considerable expertise. Tijl Capoen of Ieper kindly provided me with a photograph of the Last Post ceremony at the Menin Gate. At Poperinge, Annelies Vermeulen and Dries Chaerle from Talbot House and the staff of the Town Tourist Office all helped with the provision of photographs from their archives, and Beatrijs Osteux-Beernaert of the Hotel Palace not only provided warm hospitality at the town's leading hotel but also much local information. Other helpers were Franky D'Haene of Gullegem and Jef Hoornaert of Westouter who, between them, provided a tall step-ladder that enabled a photograph to be taken of the long line of graves at the side of Dranoutre Churchyard. Andre Decrock of Lijssenthoek gave valuable help with the background of Lijssenthoek Military Cemetery. Mevr. Jacqueline Wullus-Larmuseau of Ieper, whose father was the last doctor at the 'Doctor's House' at Kemmel, provided details of the 1914 doctor there, and Pol Vandermarliere-Pattyn of the Richelieu Restaurant on that site made me welcome there and was very helpful. Finally, Jeremy Gee, Director of the Commonwealth War Graves Commission's Northern Area based at Ieper, saw an old friendship stretched to the utmost of reasonable limits by providing much help on a personal basis.

BIBLIOGRAPHY AND SOURCES

The War Diary of the 1/4th Lincolns (from the copy held at the Museum of Lincolnshire Life).

Officers Died in the Great War, HMSO, 1919; reprinted by Samson Books Ltd, London, 1975.

Soldiers Died in the Great War, Lincolnshire, Leicestershire, Sherwood Forester, South Staffordshire, North Staffordshire and Monmouthshire Regiments, originally HMSO, but from various recent reprints.

The Casualty Database of the Commonwealth War Graves Commission.

The History of the Lincolnshire Regiment 1914-1918, by Major General C. R. Simpson, The Medici Society, 1931.

A History of 5th Battalion The Lincolnshire Regiment, by Colonel T. E. Sandall, Blackwell, Oxford, 1922.

Footprints of the 1/4th Leicestershire Regiment August 1914-November 1918, by John Milne, Backus, Leicester, 1935.

The Fifth Leicestershire, Captain J. D. Hills, published privately at Loughborough, 1919.

The War History of the Sixth Battalion The South Staffordshire Regiment, by a committee of officers, Heinemann, London, 1924.

5th Battalion The Sherwood Foresters War History 1914-1918, by L. W. de Grave, Bemrose, Derby, 1930.

The Sherwood Foresters in the Great War, The Robin Hoods, 1/7th, 2/7th, 3/7th Battalions, by officers of the battalions, Bell, Nottingham, 1921.

The Sherwood Foresters in the Great War, 1/8th Battalion, by Captain W. C. C. Weetman, Forman, Nottingham, 1920.

History of the 5th North Staffords 1914-1918, by Lieutenant Walter Meakin, Hughes and Harber, Longton.

A Town Remembers, The Boston War Memorial, Volume 1, by Dr William M. Hunt, Richard Kay Publications, Boston, 1999.

Boston at War, by Martin Middlebrook, History of Boston Project, 1974.

Boston, Its Story and People, by George S. Bagley, published jointly by the author and The History of Boston Project, 1986.

Diaries of Lance Corporals Noel Gardiner and William Kent, letters of Lieutenant Charles Ellwood.

Copies of the Boston edition of the *Lincolnshire Standard* for 1913, 1914 and 1915 held in the archives of Boston Public Library.

INDEX

(Soldiers' ranks shown are those known or believed to have been reached during the period covered by this book.)